3 -

THE
HOMEFRONT
IN
CIVIL WAR
MISSOURI

THE
HOMEFRONT
IN
CIVIL WAR
MISSOURI

JAMES W. ERWIN

THE
History
PRESS

Published by The History Press
Charleston, SC 29403
www.historypress.net

Copyright © 2014 by James Erwin
All rights reserved

Cover images: Sheet music cover for the Grand March composed for the Mississippi Valley
Sanitary Fair of 1864. *Courtesy Library of Congress*; Photo of George Maddox from Wilson's
Creek National Battlefield; Union envelope, "Poor deluded Miss-Souri takes a secession
bath." *Courtesy Library of Congress*.

First published 2014

Manufactured in the United States

ISBN 978.1.62619.433.5

Library of Congress CIP data applied for.

CONTENTS

ACKNOWLEDGEMENTS

This book does not pretend to exhaust the subject. To the contrary, it barely scratches the surface. A separate book could be written about virtually every topic and many of the individuals covered here. I have relied heavily on the work of Louis S. Gerteis and William E. Parrish, as well as the other works listed in the bibliography that provide the detail that word limits preclude here. I urge you to consult them; you will find them as fascinating as I did. I do hope the readers will find the stories selected for this book illustrative of the experiences of thousands of Missourians who had to live through the terrible time that was the Civil War.

Once again, I wish to thank Ben Gibson and the folks at The History Press for the opportunity to continue to publish works about the Civil War in my home state. I also wish to thank the following persons from the National Park Service for their assistance and suggestions: Deborah S. Wood, museum curator at Wilson's Creek National Battlefield; Karen Maxville, Ulysses S. Grant National Historic Site; and Curtis Gregory, park ranger, George Washington Carver National Monument. I am especially indebted to Wicky Sleight and Andrea Hatfield at the Marshall Missouri Public Library for their help in finding information about Elvira Scott. I also appreciate the quick response by Polly at the Kingdom of Callaway Historical Society for material on Jefferson Jones. My thanks go to Sally Conrad and Kathleen Macknicki for a photograph of Rachel King Anderson and permission to quote from her diary. And finally, a hat tip to Peggy Curran for suggesting the topic.

Finally, I can never say enough to show the appreciation or debt I owe to my wife, Vicki. She has provided needed encouragement throughout this entire project. And she has shown remarkable patience in putting up with the clutter of books, files, papers, DVDs, note cards, scribbled scraps of paper and all manner of junk that has taken over the dining room table while this book was in preparation.

PROLOGUE

Thank God the war was over.

Moses Carver came to Southwest Missouri in 1843. The Preemption Act of 1841 allowed him to buy 240 acres of the choicest land in Newton County, with timber, prairie, two springs and a creek nearby, for only $1.25 an acre. By the time the war started, Moses and his wife, Susan, had improved the property until it was one of the most valuable in the area. Like most Missourians, he did not raise only cash crops for sale. Rather, Carver grew wheat, oats, potatoes, hay and flax. Carver had a reputation as an eccentric and aloof neighbor. He cultivated bees and bred racehorses. The locals said he even had a special way with the animals—roosters sat on his shoulders and squirrels ate from his hand. He was also known as a "good fiddler."

The Carvers had no children. As they grew older, they needed help to run the farm. Although he had a white hired hand, Carver bought a slave woman named Mary from a neighbor. Carver was neither a fire-eating slaveholder nor a dedicated abolitionist. He disapproved of slavery, but it was difficult to find white men who would stay on a farm for any length of time, and certainly there were few, if any, white women who would hire out as domestics.

Mary gave birth to two boys. Their father was likely a man living on a neighboring farm. The older boy, Jim, was born in October 1859. The younger boy, George, was born in late 1864 or the spring of 1865—as with many slaves, the exact date was not recorded.

Although a slave owner, Carver was a Unionist. That was not easy living in Newton County. Carver's corner of Missouri lay on the path of

Moses Carver. *George Washington Carver National Monument.*

Confederate and Union armies as they fought for control of the state. Pro-Southern governor Claiborne Jackson and a rump legislature that escaped from Jefferson City in 1861 met just a few miles away in Neosho to approve secession and entry into the Confederate States of America. Carver likely could hear the guns when the armies clashed at Newtonia, only about ten miles away.

Worse yet, Newton County also was in the heart of the guerrilla war. John Coffee and Tom Livingston, among other bushwhackers, raided back and forth across the area, chased by Federal troops. Neither side showed much patience with civilians.

Carver tried to stay out of the way of marauding or "foraging" Confederate and Union forces. He was too old to join the militia. For the most part, he succeeded in keeping a low profile. But he was not entirely successful and nearly paid for it with is life.

In late 1862, a band of guerrillas (likely on their way to winter quarters in Texas) appeared at the Carver farm. They did not want any of his livestock or food—they wanted Carver's money. Moses refused to turn it over. The guerrillas then put a rope around Moses's neck, hung him from a tree in the yard and even put hot coals to his feet. Moses still refused. Frustrated, the raiders cut him down and left.

The next day, twelve-year-old Mary Alice Rice found Carver with his feet blistered from the bushwhackers' torture. It was an image that stuck with her the rest of her life (she lived until 1949). The war was just as troubling for her as for Carver. She saw dead and wounded men as the opposing forces fought back and forth over Southwest Missouri, leaving the landscape and most of the towns devastated. Rice's own home was burned twice during the war. One day, she was trapped at school because of a firefight on the road to her home.

But in May 1865, the war was finally over. Missouri had adopted a new constitution that would free the Carver's slaves on July 4, and the Thirteenth Amendment freeing slaves everywhere was quickly being voted on by the states.

Unfortunately, the violence continued. A group of bushwhackers once again visited the Carver farm. Moses and Jim were able to hide in a brush pile, but the raiders took Mary and young George. Moses thought they may have gone to Arkansas, but as a fifty-two-year-old civilian, he was hardly in a position to track them down.

Moses turned to a former soldier, John Bentley, for help. Bentley, a carpenter born in Leicester, England, had been a sergeant in the Eighth Cavalry, Missouri State Militia (MSM). The MSM's primary mission was to hunt down guerrillas, thus freeing other troops to join Union armies fighting conventional Confederate forces elsewhere. Bentley spent part of the war as one of the regiment's "most active spies." He was captured by guerrillas in October 1862 but apparently managed to escape. Bentley's military career was sidetracked in January 1865, when he was arrested for murder, but he was released two months later, without any apparent ill effects, by order of the general commanding the district. He was mustered out in April.

Bentley disappeared into Arkansas. He returned a few days later, but he was only partially successful. Mary was nowhere to be found, perhaps even dead. Bentley was able to recover the baby. The guerrillas were either willing to give him up or abandoned him, possibly because George was a sickly boy who was suffering from the whooping cough and the croup. As a reward for finding George, Moses gave Bentley a racehorse said to be worth $300.

Moses Carver's experience—even being hung from a tree to extract information—was not unusual. After the Confederate army left Missouri, its place was taken by bands of guerrillas, recruiters seeking men to join the conventional forces in Arkansas and cavalry striking in quick raids. Mary Alice Rice's experience was not atypical either. Although guerrillas and soldiers prided themselves on the protection of women—at least white women—from violence, that supposed solicitude did not prevent them from killing their husbands and sons in front of them or looting and burning their homes. And the slave Mary's story was not uncommon. Before the war, she was not allowed to live with her husband, her children belonged to her master and her ultimate fate is unknown but likely ended in violence.

Missouri was a battleground—over one thousand engagements were fought in the state (the third most during the Civil War)—but it was also a homefront. St. Louis was a major military base and transportation center. It was filled with Union soldiers and sailors on their way south and with the sick and wounded returning north. Jefferson City was a rude, muddy town that housed an unelected and increasingly unpopular state government. Kansas City was a Union island surrounded by guerrilla strongholds. The countryside was up for grabs, suffering from the depredations of bushwhackers and soldiers alike. And Missouri was still a slave state in a war that came to be as much about emancipation as preserving the Union. It was a turbulent, dangerous place to live.

1
A Border State on the Cusp of the War

By 1855, the controversy over extension of slavery to the territories had erupted into violence along the Missouri-Kansas border. Armed bands of Missourians crossed into the new territory to vote as "residents" in elections for a delegate to Congress and for the territorial legislature.

In St. Louis, B. Gratz Brown took to the editorial pages to excoriate proslavery supporters, including the sitting United States attorney, Thomas Reynolds. Reynolds challenged Brown to a duel. Aware that Reynolds was notoriously shortsighted, Brown accepted with the stipulation that the weapons be the "common American Rifle with open sight…at eighty yards." Reynolds refused.

But the next year, Brown renewed his attacks on Reynolds. Reynolds, who was educated in Germany and spoke German, cultivated German and Irish voters who made up a substantial portion of the city's electorate. By August 1856, the country had been horrified and split by an outbreak of violence that culminated in the murder of five men near Pottawatomie Creek by John Brown and his followers. Once again, large bands of proslavery men invaded Kansas. Brown wrote an editorial in which he claimed that Reynolds "placed Germans and Irish on a level with the negroes." Thus, Brown argued, proslavery Democrats such as Reynolds were the enemies of free white labor. This was more than Reynolds could stand. He began publicly ridiculing Brown and noted that the prior year Brown had *"refused to fight* the moment he was called on to come within *visible* distance."

It was Brown who this time issued the challenge. Reynolds accepted and named the weapons as pistols at twelve paces. Because dueling was illegal in Missouri, they had to find a secret place to vindicate their honor. They found it at Selma Hall, a mansion on a bluff overlooking the Mississippi River forty miles south of St. Louis. On August 26, they faced off. Reynolds's shot hit Brown just below the knee; Brown's shot missed altogether. The "brave and honorable gentlemen" agreed that honor was satisfied.

Honor may have been satisfied, but the dispute between the factions typified by Brown and Reynolds resulted in a war with over 700,000 deaths from battle, disease and guerrilla warfare. Much of Missouri was devastated. The institution of slavery, which was the cornerstone of much of the state's agrarian economy, was gone. The steamboat was rapidly being replaced by the railroad as the dominant mode of transportation. St. Louis, once in the running to be the center of westward expansion, gave way to Chicago. Missourians, white and black, had to face a life radically changed by war.

Spottswood Rice was not a "docile" slave. Although Missouri slaveowners regarded slavery in their state as less harsh than conditions in the Deep South, it was still slavery. Slaves were still punished—sometimes by whipping—when they clashed with their owners or overseers. Rice played an important role on the tobacco plantation owned by Benjamin W. Lewis in Howard County. Lewis purchased the seventeen-year-old Rice in 1843 for $500 from the estate of John Collins. Rice was born in Virginia and likely taken to Missouri by Collins. It is possible—even probable—that Rice was separated from his family when he left Virginia or when he was sold to Lewis.

Rice was a tobacco roller, responsible for seeing that the tobacco was properly cured and for making it into twists, plugs and cigars. Yet he frequently clashed with the black overseer, who would whip him so badly that Rice's wife would sometimes have to remove his bloody clothes and salve his wounds with grease.

Missouri was born in a controversy over slavery, and the controversy intensified before and during the war. The state was admitted to the union in 1821, along with Maine, as part of the Missouri Compromise. That agreement called for the exclusion of slavery in the Louisiana Purchase territory above the 36°30' line, except for Missouri. Settlers from Kentucky and Tennessee had poured into the state in the prior decade, bringing their slaves with them. Once statehood was achieved, the new legislature put into place numerous laws protecting the institution. Many of the new residents flocked to what became known as Little Dixie, a fertile area in the central and western part of the state along the Missouri River that included the counties of Callaway, Boone, Howard, Cooper, Saline, Lafayette and Clay—seven of the ten largest slaveholding counties in the state (the others were St. Louis, Jackson and Pike Counties).

Slavery was different in Missouri. Unlike the Deep South, where most slaves lived and worked on large plantations, in Missouri most lived and worked on small farms that would hardly qualify as plantations. In Little Dixie, for example, the 1860 census showed that there were 4,340 slaveholders, of which 2,883 (66 percent) owned fewer than 20 slaves. Only a handful of owners had more than 100 slaves.

Because most slaves lived on small farms, the men were general farm hands, and the women usually performed domestic duties, in addition to helping in the fields at peak harvest and planting times. Slave children were given lesser chores to perform, such as gathering eggs from the chickens, but were pressed into duty at harvest times. Many of the small owners hired out their slaves to work for farmers in need of labor. Rice's daughter Mary, for example, was hired out by her owner at age seven to a minister as a domestic, and later she worked for a family taking care of their three children. In Rocheport, an important Missouri River port, nearly one-third of the bondspersons were hired out in 1860. Male slaves were not only hired out as farm hands, but many also were skilled tradesmen such as blacksmiths. Some owners permitted

Slave cabins and smokehouse on the farm of Abiel Leonard, a wealthy farmer and Missouri Supreme Court judge, in Fayette, Howard County. *Library of Congress.*

male slaves to work as deckhands on the steamboats that plied the Missouri and Mississippi Rivers.

Although slaves were not allowed to marry under Missouri law, they nevertheless formed familial bonds that lasted for years. Although records are woefully incomplete, Diane Mutti Burke has tracked a sample of slave marriages that shows that more than half lasted ten years or more and produced four or more children. Because most slaves lived on small farms, their marriages were so-called abroad marriages, where the husband and wife were owned by different persons and lived on different farms. The men (men usually had more freedom to roam from the farms where they lived) were allowed to visit their wives and children once or twice a week. Spottswood Rice's wife, Arry, was owned by the Digges family—prominent residents of Glasgow. Lewis allowed Rice to visit his wife on Wednesday evenings and Sundays.

In many cases, the white owners worked alongside their slaves in the fields and barns. The smaller farms grew corn and wheat, some for their own use and some for sale. Because it was relatively easy to grow, smaller farmers also planted tobacco. Pork was an important item as well. It was also easy to produce—each farmer earmarked his hogs with an elaborate combination of notches or holes (these could be registered like a trademark with the county clerk) and let the hogs run wild. As harvest time approached, farmers would round up the hogs, fatten them with corn and slaughter them. They cured the pork and prepared it for sale by salting it.

The principal cash crops were tobacco and hemp. Tobacco was simpler to cultivate compared to hemp. The fields were plowed, harrowed and manured in January and sown in the late winter and early spring. They were transplanted from the beds in May and June, then "primed" (pruned) and "topped" (cutting off the top leaf). By mid-September, the tobacco plants were ready for harvest. Slaves cut the plants, bundled them in "hands" and hung the tobacco in sheds to cure. When the leaves could be handled without breaking, they were stripped and bound together to be put into hogsheads—large barrels that held up to 1,500 pounds of tobacco. The tobacco could be cured over smoky fires. Missouri produced three types of tobacco: a fire-cured dark, nutmeg-brown leaf favored by consumers and the European trade; a thick, cinnamon-colored leaf sold to the English, Spanish and Irish; and a bright yellow leaf made into cigars.

Benjamin Lewis owned a manufacturing plant in Glasgow that had the capacity to process three million pounds of tobacco a year, either "prizing" or pressing it into hogsheads or making plugs of chewing tobacco and cigars—Spottswood Rice's job.

The production of hemp was definitely a slave's job. The seeds were planted in April, and the plants were ready for harvest in August when the stalks were ten feet high. Slaves were able to cut about one acre per day with cradle scythes. The plants were left on the ground to dry. After they dried, the plants were bundled and left to rot—the process was called "dew rotting"—and then broken into strands. The hemp could either be pressed into bales of one hundred to five hundred pounds each or made into rope, twine or bags at a ropewalk. The finished product was used to tie cotton bales and sold to plantation owners in the South. Lexington was a center of hemp and rope production.

By 1860, St. Louis was, according to historian Louis Hunter, the "principal focus of steamboat operations on the Upper Mississippi River basin" and the "commercial metropolis" of the Northwest. Founded in 1764 by Pierre Laclede, it had grown slowly in the first years of Missouri's statehood. In 1840, it was a city of 16,000; by 1860, St. Louis grew to over 160,000. While rural Missouri was dominated by a slaveholding elite, St. Louis attracted a new mercantile class from the Northeast, which was far less sympathetic to the institution of slavery. In addition, the city and the nearby counties became home to a substantial immigrant population, particularly Germans fleeing their homeland after the Revolution of 1848 to take advantage of the cheap and fertile farmland in the state. German Americans became among the staunchest supporters of the Union. They also earned the scorn and enmity of many Southern sympathizers, who believed the "Dutch" (a corruption of "Deutsch") were mercenary foreigners hardly deserving to be citizens, let alone soldiers.

Much of the reason for the city's growth was its favorable location on the Mississippi River in the middle of the nation. It was a natural stopping point for steamboats coming down the Upper Mississippi from St. Paul and up the Lower Mississippi from New Orleans. It also lay near the mouth of the Missouri River and was an important destination of steamboats on the Ohio River. Moreover, St. Louis was a convenient port for smaller boats that served the tributaries of these rivers, such as the Illinois and Osage Rivers.

In the years preceding the war, over three thousand boats landed annually at St. Louis. Its riverfront was crowded with boats, with only their bows touching the shore and sometimes with two or three boats moored behind them. The city was an important shipyard as well, with the fourth-largest center for construction of steamboats on the western rivers, after Pittsburgh, Cincinnati and Louisville.

A bird's-eye view of St. Louis, 1859. *Lithograph by A. Janicke & Co., St. Louis. Library of Congress.*

Within the state, there were several important ports. Glasgow and Brunswick were the centers of the tobacco trade. Both served a widespread backcountry from which tobacco was transported by wagon for shipment to markets. Merchants in Brunswick, located at the northernmost bend in the Missouri River, served as middlemen for shipment of goods to inland towns as far away as Chillicothe, Trenton and Milan.

Lexington and Weston were the leading ports for shipment of hemp, rope and bagging used for packing cotton bales. Hemp bales were stacked as high as a boat's upper deck, requiring it to post deckhands with buckets of water nearby in case sparks for its smokestacks caught the bales on fire.

Most of the freight going upriver consisted of mercantile goods, such as dry goods, clothing, medicines, building materials, furniture and the like. A substantial part of these items was shipped to places like Weston, Westport and St. Joseph for outfitting emigrants headed west on the Santa Fe or Oregon Trails.

The decade before the Civil War saw the construction of the first railroads in Missouri. John Marshall Clemens, a lawyer in Hannibal (and father of Samuel Clemens, aka Mark Twain), was one of the early promoters of the Hannibal & St. Joseph Railroad. Clemens died long before his dream was realized. Working east from St. Joseph and west from Hannibal, construction crews met at Chillicothe in 1859. The railroad provided the eastern connection at St. Joseph for the short-lived Pony Express, until it was replaced by the advance of technology—the telegraph. Early in the war, a narrow-gauge short line between West Quincy, Missouri, and Quincy, Illinois, was widened and extended to connect to the Hannibal & St. Joseph at Palmyra, Missouri. This shortened communications with the east even further because Quincy had a direct connection to Chicago. (No bridge spanned the Mississippi between Missouri and Illinois until after the war.)

Also in 1859, builders of the North Missouri Railroad finished part of their projected line, connecting St. Louis to the Hannibal & St. Joseph at Hudson (now Macon). The North Missouri had no bridge across the Missouri River at St. Charles. Passengers had to debark, and freight had to be unloaded, put on wagons, ferried across the river and loaded back on to railroad cars. Finally, in 1864, a ferry was established that carried freight cars across the river to St. Charles without the need to break bulk on the St. Louis County side. The railroad provided a route that was more than two hundred miles shorter than the river. Passengers could reach St. Joseph from St. Louis in a couple of days by rail. The fastest time by riverboat was seven days; river conditions could lengthen that dramatically.

Three other railroads were built west and south from St. Louis. The Pacific Railroad ran west along the south bank of the Missouri River. By 1861, it was completed as far as Warrensburg, with its ultimate destination being Kansas City—a goal it did not reach until 1865. The Southwest Branch ran from St. Louis to Rolla. The St. Louis & Iron Mountain Railroad ran southward to Ironton.

In 1860, Missouri seemed to have a bright future. It had an excellent transportation network, it was strategically placed to be a gateway for westward expansion, its agricultural prospects were good and St. Louis was already one of the major cities of the nation. But the war came, and Missouri was torn by an internal conflict that no other state had to face in the war.

The presidential election of 1860 split the country along sectional lines. Abraham Lincoln, the Republican candidate, won, carrying the states north of the Ohio River and California and Oregon. John Breckinridge, the proslavery Democratic candidate, carried eleven of the fifteen slave states. John Bell, the Constitutional Union candidate, whose slogan was "the Union as it is, and the Constitution as it is," carried three border states.

Stephen Douglas, the Northern Democratic candidate, barely carried Missouri, with 35.5 percent of the vote. Bell finished second, just a fraction of a percentage point behind Douglas. Lincoln received only 10 percent of the Missouri vote—in large part due to German votes in St. Louis. In the Missouri River counties, Lincoln's support was negligible. There was no secret ballot in Missouri until 1863. Voters announced their choice orally in front of anyone who cared to attend the polling place. As a result, those who dared to vote for Lincoln were known to everyone. In Lexington, the election judges at first refused to allow anyone to vote for Lincoln. They finally relented, and a hardy few cast their ballot for the "Black Republican." And they were promptly ostracized by the local newspaper, which suggested that it was a good time for them to leave town.

Missouri's new governor, Claiborne Fox Jackson, although he supported Douglas in the election, not so secretly favored secession. Shortly after taking office, he explored the prospect of seizing the arms and munitions at the St. Louis Arsenal. He also took the precaution of asking the legislature to turn over control of the St. Louis police force to a board appointed by the governor. Jackson promptly named proslavery men to the posts. Jackson's lieutenant governor, Thomas Reynolds (Gratz Brown's prewar dueling opponent) organized "Minute Men," a paramilitary group that pledged to take measures against the encroachment of "Northern fanaticism and the coercion of the Federal Government." Frank Blair Jr., a U.S. congressman and brother of Lincoln's postmaster general, raised his own paramilitary group in St. Louis, the "Home Guards," mostly German Americans, to counter the secessionist "Minute Men." He also successfully sought to have rabid abolitionist Nathaniel Lyon transferred to St. Louis, along with a company of regulars, to take command of the arsenal.

Frank Blair served as the Lincoln administration's principal contact in Missouri in 1861 and later as a major general in Sherman's army. *Library of Congress.*

Jackson called for election of delegates to a convention to consider secession, expecting approval. States that had already seceded sent representatives to St. Louis to convince the Missouri delegates to join them. But Missourians overwhelmingly wanted to stay in the Union, to keep slavery and to avoid war. The convention voted ninety-eight to one to remain in the Union.

War, however, could not be avoided by any single state. On April 12, 1861, Confederate forces bombarded Fort Sumter. The country's—and Missouri's—four-year nightmare began. In May, the governor ordered the militia to Camp Jackson near St. Louis, ostensibly for "training." Lyon suspected that Jackson intended to take the arsenal. On May 10, Lyon surrounded the camp and demanded its surrender. The militia gave up without a fight. But while Lyon's troops were marching the prisoners to town, someone in a crowd of civilians fired at Lyon's men. They returned the fire. Before the mêlée was over, twenty-eight persons were killed.

When news of the affair reached Jefferson City, the legislature activated the Missouri State Guard and authorized the issuance of bonds to pay for its expenses. Sterling Price, a Mexican War veteran, was named its commander.

Jackson, Price, Lyon and Blair met at the Planter's Hotel in St. Louis, but Lyon stormed out in a huff when the state officials proposed that Federal troops be confined to St. Louis. Jackson and Price returned to Jefferson City to prepare for hostilities. They were not long in coming. On June 13, Lyon landed 1,700 troops at the capital and marched on Boonville, where he defeated a small force led by John Marmaduke. The Missouri State Guard fell back to Southwest Missouri.

August found Thomas Ewing, then chief justice of the Supreme Court of the new state of Kansas, riding the train

Charles "Doc" Jennison led Kansas Cavalry that was notorious for freeing slaves in Missouri and for depredations against white Missourians. *Wilson's Creek National Battlefield.*

Hamilton Gamble led Missouri's Union provisional government from 1861 until his death in 1864. *Wilson's Creek National Battlefield.*

from Hannibal to St. Joseph, along with his wife, Ellen, and their children. Among the fellow passengers was Charles "Doc" Jennison—the leader of the notorious "Jayhawkers." Before they left, rumors spread that bushwhackers were waiting to attack the train on its way to Palmyra.

When he was told that the Missourians would shoot him, Jennison replied, "Well, I have eighteen shots for some of them," referring to the three revolvers he was carrying.

"But they will fire at you from the bushes. You will not get a chance at them."

"Oh well, I have been shot at from behind bushes before."

Ellen Ewing observed that Jennison "is a gentlemanly man, but a terror to the Missourians." Before the year was out, Jennison would lead raids into Missouri that made no distinction between Union and Southern sympathizers—living in Missouri was enough to justify burning your home and taking your horses, cows and mules and taking your slaves back to Kansas. The result was that many men, who had been at least neutral, decided to join the Confederate army or to form guerrilla bands. Although many Kansans applauded the raids, General Henry Halleck viewed Jennison's raiders as

> *no better than a band of robbers; they cross the line, rob, steal, plunder, and burn whatever they can lay their hands upon. They disgrace the name and uniform of American soldiers…A few more such raids…will make [Missouri] as unanimous against us as is Eastern Virginia.*

In the meantime, Missouri's only functioning civil government was the convention called to consider secession. That group created the Provisional

Government of Missouri to be led by Hamilton Gamble, a St. Louis lawyer who had been a judge of the Missouri Supreme Court in the 1850s (he was the lone vote in favor of Dred Scott when his case came before the court). The provisional government removed all state-wide officers and named a new lieutenant governor, treasurer and Supreme Court judges. Gamble served as governor until his death in 1864.

2

THE PROBLEM OF SLAVERY IN A LOYAL BORDER STATE

Abolitionist-minded Republicans wanted to prohibit the expansion of slavery to the territories, believing that it would eventually die out of its own accord. Even they did not believe that Congress could abolish slavery merely by legislation because it was expressly mentioned in the Constitution. There was historical precedent, however, for the freeing of slaves as a military measure to be taken against an enemy. Thus, military necessity became the wartime watchword for the emancipation of slaves.

In May 1861, three slaves owned by a Confederate colonel ran away and sought refuge at Fortress Monroe in Virginia. The commander there, Benjamin F. Butler, refused the owner's demand to return the slaves. He determined that, if as Virginia (and other slaves states) held, the slaves were property, then they could be seized and held as property of the enemy or "contraband." Congress took the initial step toward legal emancipation by affirming Butler's treatment of escaped slaves by passage of the First Confiscation Act. This statute provided that, if any slave's labor or service was used to support the rebellion, then "the person to whom such labor or service is claimed to be due shall forfeit his claim to such labor, any law of the State or of the United States to the contrary notwithstanding."

The causes of the war have been debated since 1861. Lost Cause advocates claimed that the South seceded to protect state's rights. Of course, the "state's right" they sought to protect was slavery. Recently, historians have argued that the Union soldiers enlisted and died in the thousands to protect the Union, not to destroy slavery. Union politicians also saw preservation of the Union as the principal war aim. Even Senator James Lane, the well-known abolitionist from Kansas, disavowed any intent to fight the war as one against slavery. But as Senator Andrew Johnson noted, "If slavery shall be abolished, shall be overthrown as a consequence of this war, I shall not shed a tear over that result; but sir, it is not the purpose of the Government to prosecute this war for the purpose of overthrowing slavery. If it comes as a consequence, let it come; but it is not an end of the war."

Regardless of the views of *white* citizens, *white* politicians or *white* soldiers concerning the causes of the war or the Union's war aims, *black* Americans, including slaves in Missouri, saw the war as their opportunity for freedom. At first a trickle and later a flood of slaves escaped from their masters—loyal and disloyal—and fled to the Union armies.

Within a month after the surrender of Fort Sumter, the Union commander in Missouri wrote that he "entertain[ed] no doubt" that the United States government would protect "negro property" and that he was "not a little astonished that such a question could be seriously put." That would quickly change. As regiments from free states flowed into Missouri to protect its railroad lines and to prepare for campaigns against the Confederacy, complaints began to flood into Union headquarters in St. Louis that these soldiers were seizing slaves and refusing to return runaways to their masters.

The department's new commander, John C. Frémont, was faced with other mounting troubles. Nathaniel Lyon's army was defeated at Wilson's Creek on August 10 and Lyon himself killed. The remnants of his forces fell back to Rolla. Price was on the move to the Missouri River. Guerrillas plagued northern Missouri with attacks on trains and bridges, scurrying back to their homes and businesses to hide from pursuing Federal troops. Frémont sat at his desk to compose a proclamation that would cause a national uproar.

Frémont's August 30 edict declared martial law throughout the state. He further announced that anyone found guilty of bearing arms inside Union lines would be shot. Any persons who were found to have destroyed railroad or telegraph lines would also "suffer the extreme penalty of the law." If Frémont had stopped with those measures, despite their harshness, his proclamation might have been met with approval, at least from loyal Missourians. But he did not stop there. Frémont also declared that the real and personal property of all persons in rebellion "is declared to be confiscated for public use, *and their slaves, if any they have, are hereby declared freemen*" (emphasis added).

President Lincoln and Governor Gamble were both taken by surprise—they both learned of Frémont's actions in the newspaper. While the Republican press hailed the proclamation as a "bold step" and a "heavy blow" to the Rebels,

John C. Frémont created a national controversy in his attempt to free the slaves of persons in rebellion in 1861. *Library of Congress.*

Gamble, and more importantly, the president had a far different reaction. Lincoln was trying to keep Kentucky loyal. It had pursued an uneasy neutrality to that point, but Lincoln worried that Frémont's declaration might throw the state to the Confederacy. Moreover, as James Oakes pointed out, Frémont made a political, not a military, decision in attempting to free the slaves in Missouri. Even military necessity did not authorize soldiers to decide political issues. Moreover, the proclamation went beyond what Congress had authorized in the First Confiscation Act because it purported to free the slaves of all persons in rebellion regardless of whether the slaves had been used to support the rebellion by building fortifications, acting as teamsters and the like. Merely serving in the Confederate army, for example, was not sufficient for an owner's slaves to be freed under the First Confiscation Act.

Not wishing to embarrass his party's first presidential nominee, Lincoln wrote Frémont privately about two points that "give me some anxiety." First, Lincoln insisted that no one be executed without his express approval. Second, he noted that the provision regarding slaves "will alarm our

Southern friends and turn them against us; perhaps ruin our rather fair prospect in Kentucky." He asked that Frémont, of his "own motion," modify that paragraph to conform to the First Confiscation Act. Lincoln noted that he wrote "in a spirit of caution and not censure."

Frémont replied a few days later. He justified his failure to consult the president, or anyone else, by claiming that the rapid change of events precluded any prior notice and by the desire not to burden Lincoln because it "would demand too much of your time." He refused to rescind the order freeing the slaves unless Lincoln agreed to "openly direct me to make the correction." He would accept the "implied censure" but would not voluntarily retract it because it would suggest that he had failed to give the matter adequate deliberation and that it would further suggest that he believed it was wrong. Lincoln took Frémont's defiance in stride (although he had a tense confrontation with Frémont's wife, Jessie Benton Frémont, who had rushed to Washington to defend her husband). He "very cheerfully" and publicly ordered Frémont to revise his proclamation to conform to congressional direction.

Lincoln's order rescinding Frémont's "Missouri emancipation" did not clarify matters for Union commanders. There was still great confusion about what to do with escaped slaves. Some who had provided important military intelligence were allowed to go to St. Louis for safety. Others still fled to Union camps seeking refuge and were permitted to stay, depending in large part on the local commander's proclivities, regardless of the Confiscation Act.

After Frémont was removed, his replacement, General Henry Halleck, issued General Order No. 3 providing that no runaway slaves be allowed to enter Federal camps or join troops on the march and that any who were already there "be immediately excluded therefrom." This order created nearly as many problems as it solved. One officer, writing from Rolla, pointed out that the fugitives in his camp were acting as officer's servants, teamsters and hospital attendants. He asked that headquarters clarify whether these men and women should be expelled. Halleck replied that General Order No. 3 did not apply to persons "authorized" to be in camps, such as officer's servants. It was intended "to prevent any person in the Army from acting in the capacity as a negro catcher, or negro stealer." Military officers were not authorized to determine any matter between a slave and his purported master, except as provided by Congress in the First Confiscation Act.

At about the same time, Halleck's provost marshal reported that there were sixteen fugitive slaves being held in the St. Louis jail who had been taken by Union forces in Southwest Missouri and who were reported to

Henry Halleck tried with limited success to keep the army out of entanglements involving the catching and return of escaped slaves. *Library of Congress.*

have been used by their owners against United States forces or whose owners were reported to be in the Rebel army. Under Missouri law, these slaves were subject to being sold at auction by the sheriff because they had run away, and their owners had not claimed them within ninety days. Halleck directed that the slaves be released. Holding the fugitives was, in his opinion, contrary to the provisions of the First Confiscation Act calling for the forfeiture of the owners' right to their labor. Owners who sought to enforce their property rights, if any, had to do so in loyal state courts. The military was to "avoid all interference with such questions." Leaving Confederates to seek vindication of their rights in the civil courts controlled by the Union of course meant, as a practical matter, that they would not recover their slaves. But it also meant that the military would not be involved in the odious task of imprisoning fugitive slaves to await such an action that likely was not to come. The men in the city jail were put to work for the military to pay off the cost of their clothing and other necessities.

The legal status of escaped slaves and humanitarian concerns for their welfare plagued military and civil leaders alike in Missouri for the next four years.

3

DISPENSING AND DISPENSING WITH
JUSTICE IN A GUERRILLA WAR

In 1859 Jefferson Jones, a prominent lawyer, completed his dream home in northern Callaway County. He lived with his wife and nine children (three of whom were named Southwest, Northeast and Octave) in a two-story Southern-style plantation house with a cupola from which the 250-pound Jones—newspapers called him "our ponderous friend"—could survey his farm and twenty slaves. Jones favored secession but failed in his bid for election to the 1861 convention called by Governor Jackson.

In October 1861, Jones was alerted by a local minuteman group known as the "A to Z's" that Union Home Guards under John B. Henderson (later a United States senator and co-author of the Thirteenth Amendment) had arrived in Callaway County and were arresting suspected Secessionists. Many of those who escaped arrest gathered in the center of the county and elected Jefferson Jones as their colonel. Jones later claimed that he and his men "did not belong to army of the Southern Confederacy & did not desire to belong but that rather than yield our constitutional rights, we were determined to yield our lives." Realizing that his rabble was no match even for the poorly equipped Home Guards, Jones met with Henderson to reach a truce. Their agreement—later called a "treaty" by Southern enthusiasts—provided that Jones's men would disband in return for a promise that Henderson would respect their constitutional rights. Jones said that he met with General John Schofield, the local Union commander several times, and that Schofield approved the agreement with Henderson. This agreement would later be the basis for the claim that the Union recognized the "Kingdom of Callaway."

Jefferson Jones negotiated an agreement with John Henderson that became the basis for the legend of the Kingdom of Callaway. *Kingdom of Callaway Historical Society.*

Senator John B. Henderson, an early advocate of gradual emancipation, played a key role in the adoption of the Thirteenth Amendment. *Library of Congress.*

Had matters ended there, Jones might have had a much less turbulent Civil War. But Jones was unable to restrain his opposition to Union forces whom he regarded, along with many Secessionist sympathizers, as invaders. General Sterling Price issued orders in December 1861 that an attack should be made on the North Missouri Railroad. Among the leaders of the Rebel forces was a Lieutenant Jamison, Jones's nephew. Their task was to burn the railroad's bridges and tear up its track. They met at Jones's farm on December 20. Union forces got wind of the attack and deployed troops to prevent it. They were not entirely successful, as the Rebels did $160,000 in damages in destroying bridges, buildings and track. But the Federals were more successful in capturing the culprits.

Although Jones himself did not participate in the raid, he was arrested and charged with aiding and abetting the destruction of the railroad, aiding and abetting insurrection and acting as a spy and holding unlawful communications with the enemy. He sat in jail for a month and was finally released on January 27, 1862, upon posting a bond. While he was confined, Union soldiers—Jayhawkers, Jones claimed—burned the mill on his property, insulted his family and stole his wagons, horses and mules, their saddles, blankets, chains and other equipment. The soldiers also took five bolts of "negro shirting" that left his slaves without new clothes for the winter. Jones put all of these complaints into a letter to General Schofield, whom he apparently regarded as some sort of champion to whom he could appeal. Jones was mistaken. Schofield replied coldly that he had "no doubt you have suffered much inconvenience" but that all he would be made to suffer "will fall short of atoning for the misery caused by you not only to Union men but to the misguided dupes who have yielded to your baneful influence," the "evil effect" of which "can hardly be counterbalanced by the loss of a few wagons and horses." Schofield nevertheless promised Jones a fair trial and said, "I should be gratified if you are found less guilty than I believe you to be."

Later that year, Jones got his trial before a military commission sitting in Danville. Jones provided a skillful defense. Even the captured guerrillas who testified against him conceded that he told them he did not want men there who might lead to his arrest. Jones explained that a large cache of who and ammunition found at his home was purchased in bulk so that he would not have to be "piddling so often with the stores." Jones asserted that he respected the agreement with Henderson and had not taken up arms against the government and had not willingly cooperated with the Rebels. He was acquitted on all charges. But apparently reflecting the unproven suspicions surrounding his conduct, Jones was required to sign an oath of allegiance and to post a $10,000 bond to secure "future good conduct."

For the moment, Jones escaped the wrath of Federal justice. But he was far from disentangled from it. In 1863, a Unionist neighbor, Dr. James Martien, wrote to Union authorities requesting that they investigate Jones for renewed secessionist activities. A Union scout, William Poillon, gathered evidence that Jones had secretly supported Confederate recruiter Colonel Joseph Porter and the notorious guerrilla Alvin Cobb the prior year. Jones asserted that Dr. Martien had a personal grudge because Jones had successfully sued him for unpaid attorney's fees and because Jones's father-in-law had obtained a writ against Martien for return of a slave who had run away. The authorities found that Jones had violated his bond and who a sale of his property. Jones's friends tore down the signs and prevented any sale. Major Daniel Draper, the local commander, wrote that "Rebels and rebel sympathizers all through the country are to-day rejoicing." Rather surprisingly, Federal officials allowed Jones to leave Missouri in 1864 to visit several states in the East and Midwest to buy sheep for his farm. Upon his return, Jones was accused of spying and belonging to a "secret agency." Once again, Jones was jailed. He became ill and reportedly lost nearly one hundred pounds. He remained in confinement until released in 1865.

The experience of Jefferson Jones was not uncommon. Many of those captured in December 1861 were brought before military commissions charged not only with bridge burning but also with violations of the laws of war and even treason. The legal basis for these charges was shaky. Certainly, they burned bridges, but railroad bridges were a legitimate military target, and many defendants asserted that they had done so under orders from General Price. These pleas went nowhere despite evidence produced by some defendants of their military commissions from Rebel forces. The defense appears to have failed because they were not formally mustered into Confederate service and lacked uniforms—a most peculiar rationale given that most of the Confederate army in Missouri had no uniforms either. And treason is an offense whose elements and standard of proof is specifically defined in the Constitution. Even Halleck, who otherwise approved of military commissions, drew the line at allowing military tribunals to hear charges of treason because such crimes were properly for the civil courts.

Two parts of Frémont's August 30 proclamation were not modified by Lincoln: the plan to give military authorities the power to try civilians for violations of existing laws and to "supply such deficiencies as the conditions of war demand" and the declaration of martial law throughout the state. The establishment of military commissions found its precedent in the Mexican War. During that conflict, General Winfield Scott found that the occupying forces of the United States Army—particularly, in his view, the volunteers— were committing what would otherwise be deemed crimes under civil law, such as murder, rape and robbery of Mexican civilians, but they were not subject to punishment by military law. Accordingly, he devised a system of military commissions to try these offenses, primarily committed by his own troops. His actions shocked his superiors, but they did nothing to stop him. In 1861, his innovation was adapted to a civil war.

The first commissions began to try defendants in September 1861 and continued even after the war was over. Military commissions were active throughout the United States, even in states as far away from the active conflict as Massachusetts (site of Fort Warren in Boston) and Wisconsin (where, albeit, only one such trial was held). Missouri had the most trials by military commissions by a comfortable margin. Mark Neely found there were 4,271 trials by military commissions. Of these, the location of the trial could be determined in 4,203 cases—and of these, 1,940, or 46.2 percent, were held in Missouri.

Nonetheless, conviction was not a foregone conclusion, as Jefferson Jones's case demonstrated. After an early acquittal rate of 15 percent, the rate of "not guilty" verdicts in Missouri plummeted to only 4 percent. All of the verdicts were reviewed by higher authorities (Lincoln, as noted above, insisted on reviewing all death sentences), and the sentences were frequently mitigated to imprisonment, a lesser term of imprisonment or a fine.

Officers reviewing commission proceedings insisted that they follow procedures for courts-martial under the Articles of War. For example, the commission had to consist of at least three officers, there had to be an officer designated as the judge advocate to prosecute the case and proceedings had to be recorded. Indeed, the records of the military commissions were, in many instances, more complete than civil criminal trials in many states. The failure to swear the commission "in the presence of the accused" or the failure of the record to indicate that it had been done, was sufficient error to require reversal. Some of the charges were thrown out as too "informal" because volunteer or militia officers drawing them up failed to follow court-martial form, which required them to consist of two parts: the charge describing the offense and at least one specification detailing the facts supporting the charge, i.e., "the act, time, place and circumstance." In some cases, the commission found the defendant guilty of the charge but not the specification, which rendered the conviction void because without a guilty verdict on the underlying facts the accused could not be guilty of the offense.

The accused was entitled to counsel of his or her choice, at least within limits. Isaac Snedecor, a Union officer, named his cousin, none other than Jefferson Jones, as a witness for his trial. But authorities found out that was merely a pretext under which Jones was secretly providing legal counsel to Snedecor, and prohibited Jones from further participation in the proceedings. The defendant's attorney, consistent with court-martial practice of the time, could not question or cross examine witnesses—that could be done only by the accused—but he was allowed to be present, offer advice and provide legal briefs or memoranda the accused could submit to the commission. (Snedecor, incidentally, was acquitted. The trial was so poorly conducted—not a single witness had any pertinent knowledge of the charges—that the department judge advocate scolded those involved for their inadequate preparation and complained that "due inquiry would have disclosed this and prevent the necessity of arraignment of the prisoner.")

The commissions were not supposed to accept affidavits in lieu of live testimony. The defendant was allowed to have witnesses produced. This requirement sometimes resulted in long delays or adjournment of the proceedings because the witnesses were not available (military witnesses may be on duty in remote areas of the state) or had to travel from their homes to the place of trial.

The offenses tried by military commissions usually involved men charged with participating in guerrilla activities, including murder, burning of homes, looting or attack on Union soldiers, but even seemingly innocuous activities could bring a person before a commission to face drastic punishment. Neely cites the cases of James Sullivan and Elbert Rankin, who were found guilty of disloyal conduct. Sullivan had proclaimed, "I am a Jeff Davis man," and Rankin had said "I am a Rebel" and took payment for a mule in Confederate money. Even writing to a loved one could be a crime under military law. James Jackson was convicted of writing his son, a soldier in the Confederate army. His sentence was reduced to the posting of a bond because the reviewing officer found him to be of advanced age and ignorant of military law in such instances.

Military commissions handed down punishments ranging from death sentences to imprisonment, banishment or, as in the case of James Jackson, the posting of a bond. The death sentences were reserved for suspected guerrillas who were convicted of the most serious offenses. The commission's sentence was reviewed by departmental judge advocates and the departmental commanders. In many cases, they reduced the death penalty to imprisonment. Those that were not reduced were referred to Washington, where the case was reviewed by the army's judge advocate general, Joseph Holt, and ultimately President Lincoln. Records show that 210 cases were submitted to Lincoln, of which 184 show the action he took. Overall, Lincoln approved the sentence in 90 cases and mitigated it in 94 cases.

One of the first measures the Union military used to try to control guerrilla attacks without the use of force was assessments against known or suspected Southern sympathizers. Assessments were simply confiscation of property. There was no legal basis for such actions, although it differed only in degree from "foraging," a practice used by both armies to appropriate supplies from civilians under the rubric of military necessity. The theory behind assessments was that they would discourage disloyal citizens from providing help to guerrillas or Confederate forces because of the threat that their property would be seized and sold. It did not involve outright violence other than, of course, the force necessary to take the property.

General John Pope introduced the use of assessments in the summer of 1861 to stop what he called "wanton destruction" of railroad bridges. Pope issued a notice that he would hold the inhabitants of towns and villages within five miles of any destruction financially accountable unless they could provide "conclusive proof of active resistance" or "immediate information...giving names and details" to the army. He followed up with an order directing that each county seat and town appoint "the leading State-rights men (secessionists)...to serve on committees of safety against their will, and their property...made responsible for any violence or breach of peace committed by their friends."

Although the order was intended to protect the railroads from guerrilla depredations, even railroad officials opposed it. J.T.K. Hayward, president of the Hannibal & St. Joseph, wrote to his superiors in Boston that "if we cannot have a change in the administration of military affairs here in North Missouri our cause will be ruined." A prominent lawyer from Palmyra added his warning that Pope's assessments were "exceedingly hurtful to the Union cause, in that, it gives color to the clamor of secessionists that the government is oppressive and that the purpose of the war is subjugation of the state and the South."

Citizens did their best to avoid being named to one of the committees. William "Uncle Billy" Martin, an ardent and wealthy secessionist from Audrain County, sought help from his friend Isaac Sturgeon. Sturgeon was not only the Unionist president of the North Missouri Railroad, but he was also married to Pope's niece. Together they went to see Pope at his headquarters in Mexico, Missouri. Sturgeon, however, failed to back up Martin's plea to be let off the committee, pointing out to Pope that "if I had a matter I wanted well attended to, Uncle Billy would be *the* man I would select." Martin was heard to mutter as he left, "I never imagined I would be an officeholder under Abe Lincoln." Shortly afterward, Frémont, bowing to pressure from Unionists and railroad officials, intervened to disband the committees.

Pope's less than satisfactory experience with assessments did not deter Federal commanders from using them again. In late 1861, St. Louis was flooded with refugees, mostly fleeing from the Confederate forces in Southwest Missouri—perhaps as many as forty thousand men, women and children, both white and black. The new commander in Missouri, Henry Halleck, wrote: "Men, women and children have alike been stripped and

William "Uncle Billy" Martin unsuccessfully tried to avoid serving on General John Pope's committee of public safety. From Herschel Schooley, *Centennial History of Audrain County*.

plundered. Thousands of such persons are finding their way to this city barefooted, half clad, and in a destitute and starving condition."

On December 12, Halleck issued General Order No. 24, which provided for the assessment of persons to pay for the cost of feeding, clothing and housing the refugees. Some three hundred persons were named as being subject to the levy. On Christmas Eve, the first assessments were issued to sixty persons. A few protested their loyalty and appealed. Others were defiant and "declared that they would see their houses burned over their heads before paying one cent."

In response to the complaints, Halleck appointed a new board of assessors. The board assessed a total of $16,340 against St. Louis citizens—over their renewed protests. Franklin Dick, one of the assessors, wrote in his journal that the targets of the assessments "neither appeal nor pay. I am inclined to think that Genl. Halleck will have to resort to Extreme measures with them." A week later, he wrote that Union authorities were "seizing the chattels of the assessed Traitors in the City & they are howling in suppressed tones."

Samuel Engler sought redress in the civil courts. He obtained a court order directing that the provost marshal return twenty-nine boxes of Admantine candles and fifty-one boxes of Star candles. He took Sheriff John Andrews with him to serve the writ and regain possession of his property. The guard refused. The local paper reported: "The Sheriff concluded that his duty did not require him to be absolutely riddled with Minié balls and to sacrifice the lives of his undisciplined corps, and therefore gracefully ordered a retreat." Andrews's return on the writ was less colorful but succinct: he failed to execute the court order because of "an armed body of men purporting to act under the authority of the United States which force it was not possible for me to resist or overcome."

Halleck reacted immediately to Engler's presumption by arresting him and his attorney. Dick gleefully reported that an armed guard escorted Engler out of town. After posting a bond, Engler was allowed to return to St. Louis later in the year. But he was banished in May 1863 for making disloyal statements.

In February 1862, the authorities auctioned the seized goods. The *St. Louis Republican* described the scene:

> *An immense crowd, more than could obtain entrance, was present yesterday morning, and only those who went early could secure places inside. So great was the rush, that it was found necessary to detail a squad of soldiers to keep the sidewalks clear and preserve an open ingress and egress.*
>
> *A large number of ladies were present, and many having been wedged in by the throng, found it difficult to extricate themselves when they wished, and were compelled to stand upon the wet and sloppy floor—a situation the reverse of comfortable. Some secession sympathizers found their way into the rooms, and by a variety of sneers and mutterings, bid fair at times to interrupt "the perfect harmony of the occasion"; but, as a usual thing, there was less disorder and confusion than might have been expected.*
>
> *As a general thing, considering the times, the furniture, &c., brought fair prices, though in some instances great bargains were had. An elegant piano, nearly new, said to have cost Mr. KAYSER between $500 and $600 in Europe, was sold for $240. Another, for which Mr. POLK is*

reputed to have given over a $1,000, went for $330. A set of brocatel rosewood furniture, (sofa, arm chairs, and fancy chairs,) owned by Mr. PARK, brought $145. A lot of miscellaneous books, one hundred and ten in number, the property of Mr. FUNKHOUSER, netted about $29. Some of the line carpets, velvet and Brussels, were sold low, while others brought full retail prices.

The provost marshal, in a show of punctiliousness, found that Engler's property sold for more than he owed, and refunded him $4.97. But any apparent fairness in the auction did not mollify critics of the assessment process. Dick noted in his diary that

> *I have contracted additional hate from these bloody Traitors here by acting on this* [assessment] *Comm. & our weak knee'd Union people shake their heads at it…In St. Louis, I feel that we have in our midst a damnable, wicked & treacherous set of bloodhounds—their hatred at me for being on the Asst. Commission is deep & exasperated—and I feel pointedly the stupid weakness of Congress in permitting these Traitors to remain openly defiant & hostile here, where they do so much injury.*

The moderate success of the assessments in St. Louis in paying for refugee relief encouraged General John Schofield and Governor Gamble to resort to them later to finance the Enrolled Missouri Militia (EMM). They created the EMM to provide additional troops to fight guerrillas. Gamble agreed to pay EMM soldiers while they were on active duty, although they were subject to Federal army control. But the state had little money to spend on anything, let alone more armed forces. And so Gamble assessed St. Louis banks $150,000, with repayment to come from taxes or assessments on disloyal citizens. Schofield concurrently assessed secessionists in St. Louis County the sum of $500,000 to pay for the EMM's arms, clothing and subsistence.

The temptation to take from neighbors, whether out of spite, greed or both, was too great. Assessment boards levied sums based on mere claims that one person or another was disloyal or had made questionable statements. Within months, prominent Missouians such as William Greenleaf Eliot were urging the suspension of the program because it was shot through with errors and, inevitably, corruption. The local civil and military authorities disclaimed any attempt to rectify the situation, each claiming that it was the other's responsibility to do so. As with other controversies arising out of local Missouri squabbles, the matter worked its way to the president's desk. Lincoln suspended the policy in December, and in January 1863, the War Department ended it altogether.

Or so it thought. Several commanders in the field decided that the policy was too valuable to comply with presidential orders and continued to make assessments against suspected Rebels. Some, like arch radical Benjamin Loan, suggested that those assessed could make a "donation" if they chose—as long as they paid.

Union commanders once again resorted to assessments in 1864, but General William Rosecrans limited them to pay for specific cases where the head of a family had been killed or wounded by guerrillas or the Confederate army. In one instance, Rosecrans revived the Pope assessments and collected the cost of repairing a railroad bridge over the Salt River from Monroe and Shelby Counties. To the anger of Radical Republicans, Rosecrans refused to assess secessionists to pay for the cost of providing relief to the thousands of persons who fled to St. Louis in the fall of 1864 to escape the guerrillas and Price's invading army. General Grenville Dodge, who replaced Rosecrans, was more favorably disposed to assessments and did allow some to be made against the property of known secessionists to pay for renovations to a hospital. But by February 1865, Lincoln had again suspended the program. With the lifting of martial law in March and the end of the war in April, the assessment of citizens finally stopped.

As a policy to stop or discourage guerrilla warfare in the state, assessments were, as W. Wayne Smith said, "a distinct failure." As a method of financing refugee relief, assessments were effective in raising needed funds. But in both situations, assessments caused deep-seated resentment. And like many harsh Union policies, they only entrenched secessionists in their hatred of the federal government—a hatred that was exacerbated by perceived (and in many cases, accurate) notions that the assessments were the result of revenge, abuse and corruption.

4

Missouri as Military Base

In January 1860, the St. Louis Arsenal had sixty thousand muskets, ninety thousand pounds of powder, 1.5 million ball cartridges, forty cannons and machinery to manufacture weapons. That alone would have made it important for either the North or the South to control the city. The city's location midway between the Upper Midwest and the Gulf made it the most important port on the Mississippi River after New Orleans. It was also a center of rail transportation, with lines emanating to the northwest, west, southwest and south.

Missouri bordered two Confederate states (Arkansas and Tennessee) and one key border state (Kentucky) and sat between four free states (Illinois, Iowa, Kansas and Nebraska). The principal water route to the Northwest—the Missouri River—crossed the state's center. Its northern rail network, particularly the Hannibal & St. Joseph, provided the only rail link between the Mississippi and the Missouri Rivers. Missouri was, in short, a vital strategic base for the Western, Trans-Mississippi and Northwest Theaters.

Nathaniel Lyon's aggressive actions at Camp Jackson were (and in some quarters still are) considered imprudent and the catalyst for plunging Missouri into the midst of a bloody civil war. But there was simply no way that it could remain neutral, regardless of many citizens' wishes to do so.

By August 1861, troops had begun to pour into St. Louis. General Frémont rented 150 acres on the northwest edge of St. Louis for a "camp of instruction." It was first named Camp Benton, to honor Missouri senator Thomas Hart Benton (General Frémont's father-in-law). It later became

Second Wisconsin Cavalry at Benton Barracks in 1862. The headquarters building can be seen in the background. *Wilson's Creek National Battlefield.*

known as Benton Barracks. Frémont had five rows of barracks constructed, each 740 feet long and 40 feet wide. The quarters of each company were separated by partitions, and there was a separate company kitchen with brick furnaces on which to cook in back. There were soon added warehouses, stables and a two-story administration building. It had few trees and a large, bare parade ground that became a quagmire of mud when it rained. But the area was well drained, and the parade grounds dried quickly. The post was low enough that pipes were run from the city's reservoirs to the kitchens.

Although soldiers described the buildings as comfortable and well designed—at least as compared to the rude camps many of them initially occupied upon enlistment—the winter of 1861–62 soon proved otherwise. An epidemic of measles swept through the base, killing a number of men. The Western Sanitary Commission, which was organized to provide medical and other services to wounded and sick soldiers and refugees, criticized conditions at Benton Barracks:

> *The presence of so many troops in one great encampment, the crowded condition of the barracks, the inexperience of the soldiers in their first encounter with exposure and hardship, the inclemency of the winter months, and the inability of the department to do all that was required, occasioned a*

large amount of sickness among the different regiments. The most prevalent diseases were measles, pneumonia, typhoid fever, and diarrhea. In one instance, it happened that three hundred, in a single regiment of cavalry, were sick, mostly taken down with measles. In another, the surgeon reported one thousand out of thirteen hundred men, suffering from coughs and colds. The barracks being rough buildings, with many open cracks, and floors without any space beneath, were far from comfortable, and the regimental hospitals were not well warmed, nor kept at an even temperature, nor properly ventilated. The consequence was that many of the measle patients were afterwards attacked with pneumonia, and died.

Two of its early commanders were Samuel Curtis and William T. Sherman. Both served there only a short time before receiving field commands. Colonel Benjamin L.E. Bonneville was the commander during most of the time Benton Barracks was active. Bonneville was a distinguished western explorer in his younger days but was now, as one recruit described him, "a little dried-up old Frenchman…[with] no military look about him whatever."

In short order, regiments from Illinois, Indiana, Iowa, Ohio, Wisconsin, Minnesota and Missouri arrived at Benton Barracks to be trained and equipped. By April 1862, there were about twenty-three thousand men at Benton Barracks. Drilling was boring work, particularly early in the war when many units had no weapons. The first regiment—the Second Missouri Volunteer Cavalry—left in September 1861. It began patrolling in Central Missouri that fall, and by December, it had clashed with a large body of Confederate cavalry led by Jo Shelby near Waverly. Most of the rest left in the late spring or early summer of 1862, as commanders demanded more men be sent to the front.

Benton Barracks became the largest military hospital in the area, with one thousand beds for convalescent patients. It also became a camp for paroled prisoners. Prisoners of war could be taken back to a prison camp, such as that at Elmira, New York (for Confederate prisoners) or at Andersonville, Georgia (for Union prisoners). There they would be kept until exchanged. As a more practical alternative for the capturing forces—because it put the burden of caring and accounting for the men on the prisoners' own army—the men could be paroled. They were issued documents signifying their capture and sent back to their own lines or left for their own forces to pick them up. Paroled men could not serve in any military capacity until they were exchanged for a like number of men of equivalent rank.

At first, paroled Union prisoners were allowed to go home to wait orders to report back to their units when exchanged. That system quickly became abused for obvious reasons, and Union commanders then sent the men to special camps for parolees. There were three such camps at Benton Barracks.

If drilling was boring, being in one of the battalions of parolees was even worse. The Seventy-eighth Illinois Infantry Regiment had two whole companies captured by John Hunt Morgan on a raid into Kentucky in December 1862. They were sent en masse to Benton Barracks to await exchange. They spent ten months there, doing little but getting into trouble. The regiment's historian noted that the number of courts-martial for these two companies during their stay in St. Louis exceeded the number for the rest of the regiment in the entire war. Men from four Iowa regiments were ordered to perform guard duty in relief of active Missouri troops. They refused because they believed it was a violation of their parole. General Halleck countered that guard duty was not "military service" prohibited by the terms of the paroles but merely a housekeeping matter for their own good.

Perhaps some of the Seventy-eighth Illinois or Iowa parolees were involved in a soldiers' riot at Hyde Park on July 4, 1863. Soldiers and parolees from the barracks went to the nearby park to relax. Probably its most popular attraction was a bar run by a Mr. Kuhlage. On Independence Day, there was to be a hot air balloon ascension. Tickets to the event went slowly, and some of the more impatient soldiers decided not to wait. They broke down the fence and made their way into the park. This drew police and a detachment of the Second Missouri Artillery to keep the peace. In the meantime, Kuhlage tried to cool matters down by stopping the sale of beer. This naturally had the opposite effect on the thirsty soldiers, and a brawl ensued. The police stopped that fight, but another broke out a couple hours later with more deadly results. Rioting soldiers destroyed the balloon, set off the fireworks stored for the show that night and returned to Kuhlage's saloon. There they were confronted by a detail of the Second Missouri Artillery from the St. Louis city garrison. The artillery lieutenant ordered his men to fire without loading balls in their weapons, but some of the men—perhaps panicking at the approach of an unruly mob—decided to use more lethal measures. The ensuing volley killed four paroled soldiers and two civilians, both sixteen-year-old boys. A coroner's jury condemned the shootings as murder, but the men who pulled the triggers with loaded muskets were never identified, and in the end, no one was punished.

In late 1863, Benton Barracks began to fill up with another set of new recruits—African American soldiers who were mostly former slaves. They were mustered in four regiments—the Sixty-second, Sixty-fifth, Sixty-seventh and Sixty-eighth United States Colored Infantry. Like the white soldiers before them, the members of these units suffered terribly while being trained and equipped at the barracks. During the winter of 1863–64. Lieutenant Colonel William Fox reported that more than one hundred men from the Sixty-second Infantry alone died, some of them having "suffered amputation of frozen feet or hands, and the diseases engendered by this exposure resulted in a terrible and unprecedented mortality." Conditions did not get better when these troops took the field. The Sixty-second, Sixty-fifth and Sixty-seventh Regiments were sent to Morganza, Louisiana—described by a historian of the United States Colored troops as one of the unhealthiest places in the United States. In a few months, 1,374 of the original 3,158 men in the three regiments were dead.

General Frémont had ten forts built that ringed St. Louis. They were manned in 1864 to be ready to repel Price's invading army, but the Confederates got no closer to the city than the town of Pacific on the Meramec River about thirty-five miles away. The army still occupied the St. Louis Arsenal and Jefferson Barracks, although the latter had only a small garrison and was used primarily as a hospital.

The government built a United States Cavalry Corral just north of Benton Barracks in October 1863. This one-hundred-acre tract had stables, warehouses, a blacksmith shop and other buildings necessary to care for up to nine thousand horses, although no more than five thousand were present at any one time. The corral employed 950 men during its year of operation. The government bought 38,714 horses at a price of either $160 or $170 each, depending on whether they were suitable for cavalry or artillery use. In addition, another 8,563 horses were sent to the corral for rehabilitation. A total of 4,018 were successfully returned to service. The remaining horses were either sold, died of disease or were euthanized.

St. Louis was also an important supply port and naval base during the war. It provided support for Union armies in the Western and Trans-Mississippi Theaters. Civil commerce was disrupted, of course, by the closure of the Mississippi in 1861. Trade on the Missouri River remained at prewar levels through 1862 despite periodic guerrilla attacks. The *New Sam Gaty* was involved in a notorious incident on March 28, when Quantrill's men stopped it near Sibley, in eastern Jackson County. They heard that Hugh Fisher, an abolitionist minister, was supposed to be on board with freed slaves from southeast Missouri whom he was taking to Kansas. It was rumored later that a steward on the boat, D.T. Riley, may have passed the word to the guerrillas. The slaves were there, but Fisher did not make the trip. Sixty former slaves ran away in terror. The remaining twenty or so were lined up, and the guerrillas executed nine of them. They robbed the passengers and threw tons of army supplies into the river.

A drought and increased guerrilla activity depressed traffic somewhat in 1863, but business perked up in 1864. The government chartered a number of boats to take military supplies to Fort Leavenworth, for troops guarding the Santa Fe and Oregon Trails. In addition, the army, under General Alfred Sully, ramped up its campaign against Indians in the Dakota Territory. Adding to the mix of traffic was an influx of prospective miners—including many men who decided to leave Missouri for the duration of the war—to Montana for the latest gold rush.

The government undertook a major deportation as part of its efforts to protect Minnesotans, hundreds of whom had been killed in 1862 during the Dakota War. The government sent 500 Dakotas by boat from St. Paul to St. Louis, where they were transferred to another boat to take them to St. Joseph. Another 800 Dakotas and 1,900 Winnebagos went by boat to Hannibal and thence via the Hannibal & St. Joseph Railroad to St. Joseph. At that city, all 3,200 were crammed onto two boats that took thirteen days to reach their final destination.

St. Louis was not just a logistics base, but it also became a shipbuilding center for the Western Fleet, primarily due to the efforts of James B. Eads. Eads was a self-taught engineer and mathematician. At the age of eighteen, he hired on as a "mud clerk," or assistant purser, on a steamboat plying the iron trade between St. Louis and Galena, Illinois. In the mid-1840s, he designed a double-hulled snag boat to clear the hundreds of dead trees floating in the river. Eads's snag boat was also used to salvage a sunken boat's cargo and equipment (a boiler, for example, could be recovered and installed in a new boat). Eads called his snag boat a "submarine" because he devised a diving bell connected to an air hose by which a man could be lowered to the bottom of the river channel to retrieve goods. Eads was not a man who would use someone else as a guinea pig—he made numerous dives himself until lung problems (probably due to his dives) caused him to go into semi-retirement.

Shortly after the Camp Jackson Affair, Eads wrote to Secretary of the Navy Gideon Welles to propose the fortification of Cairo, Illinois, and to offer one of his snag boats for conversion to a floating battery. Eads traveled to Washington to meet Welles personally and to urge the creation of a western river fleet. He learned that the government was already working on such a

James B. Eads employed four thousand men to build ironclads for the Western Fleet at Carondelet that helped to open the Mississippi River. *Library of Congress.*

project. John Rodgers and Samuel Pook designed ironclads with rectangular upper decks protected by stout oak planking and iron plating. The government planned to build these vessels, known as "Pook's Turtles" for their shape, at Cincinnati. But Quartermaster General Montgomery C. Meigs learned from his brother-in-law Frank Blair that the Ohio River was subject to periods of low water during the summer campaign months. Eads bid the job and won a contract to build the ironclads at Carondelet, a village south of St. Louis, for $89,000 each.

The first ship, the *Carondelet*, was launched on October 12, 1861. Six more vessels followed: *St. Louis* (later *Baron DeKalb*), *Louisville*, *Pittsburg*, *Cincinnati*, *Mound City* and *Cairo*. To build these ships in such a short time required a massive effort. Eads scoured the city for artisans and at the end of the

Eads-built gunboats *Baron DeKalb* (formerly *St. Louis*), *Mound City* and *Cincinnati*. *Library of Congress.*

first two weeks had five hundred men at work around the clock. Eventually, the Carondelet boatyard employed four thousand men and boys. Eads built seven more ironclads for the Western Fleet, two of which were lighter ships for use on the Tennessee and Cumberland Rivers and the rest for use on the Lower Mississippi. Each of them had turrets instead of the "turtle" design, six of them with turrets designed by Eads as an improvement over the type used in the USS *Monitor*.

The government also had Eads convert one of his snag boats, *Submarine No. 7*, to a gunboat. The submarine had two hulls, each with seven watertight compartments, so the boat would not sink if it were penetrated by a cannon ball. For military purposes, the two hulls were joined at the deck level and below the water line. It had a superstructure similar to the Pook ironclads. When finished, the vessel became the USS *Benton*, the largest gunboat on the western waters. It served as Admiral Andrew Foote's flagship. Much of the *Benton*'s crew came from the army. In the fall of 1862, it took on a number of runaway slaves while moored at Helena, Arkansas. Many stayed on the boat to serve as firemen.

While St. Louis was the largest military base in Missouri, it was hardly the only one. Rolla was the railhead of the Southwest Branch of the Pacific

Railroad. It had two forts: Fort Wyman was rectangular with a dry moat around it; a second fort called Star Fort (presumably for its shape) was constructed in 1864. Both had emplacements for cannons. The town of six hundred had thousands of Union soldiers pass through between St. Louis and the Southwest. Supply wagon trains provided a rather tenuous link between Rolla and Springfield over the rutted and often nearly impassable Wire Road and from there to troops in northwestern Arkansas and Fort Scott, Kansas. Rachel Anderson noted in her diary that her husband was regularly pressed into duty as a teamster to take his wagon to Rolla for supplies. He was paid thirty-two dollars for the trip, which no doubt was welcome income to a family virtually trapped in their home by marauding bands that plagued Southwest Missouri during the entire war.

Once Price's army was driven out of the state in early 1862, Springfield became another armed camp. Union troops built five forts to protect the town. These were earthen redoubts surrounded by a ditch, each with places in the corners for artillery. These forts, unlike those in St. Louis, came into use when John Marmaduke led a raid into the state in January 1863. Fort No. 4, in particular, was the site of fierce fighting between Marmaduke's Missouri Confederates and elements of the Missouri State Militia, the Enrolled Missouri Militia, Iowa Infantry and the "Quinine Brigade"—about one hundred convalescents from the military hospital. Marmaduke left the next day, and Springfield was not seriously threatened again.

Another fort that saw an even fiercer battle was Fort Davidson, located near the railhead at Pilot Knob. Fort Davidson had six sloping sides, each about one hundred feet long, surrounded by a moat twelve feet wide and six feet deep. It also had a covered magazine. While a strong fortification, it was located between two tall mountains, the eponymous Pilot Knob and Shepherd Mountain. When Price attacked the fort, however, he failed to take full advantage of the favorable terrain and instead launched frontal assaults. These were repulsed with heavy losses. That night, the Federal garrison slipped past inattentive Confederate forces and made their escape. But not before blowing up the magazine in a spectacular blast that was felt twenty miles away.

In addition to forts and fortified towns, Federal troops also built blockhouses to guard important railroad bridges, such as the North Missouri bridge over Peruque Creek in St. Charles County. Isaac Sturgeon, the president of the North Missouri, was particularly concerned about this bridge, writing that if it were destroyed, "the use of our road would be at an end, as it would take several months to rebuild it." The blockhouses were strongly built two-story affairs, with rectangular upper stories set at an angle over similar rectangular first stories. They had rifle ports to give maximum protection to the defenders. The local EMM company was usually detailed to man the blockhouses when the bridge was threatened by guerrillas or raiding Confederate cavalry. For the most part, these defenses were not tested. During his 1863 raid, however, Jo Shelby routed the EMM stationed at the Lamine River blockhouse and burned the bridge and the blockhouse.

Due to the nature of guerrilla war, most Federal troops were scattered about the state in battalion, company-size or smaller posts in county seats (brick courthouses were a favorite fortification if the town was attacked) and other strategic spots. These units were moved frequently from place to place to conduct "scouts" (patrols) for guerrillas, to raid guerrilla camps or simply to sweep through areas to interrogate the inhabitants, to force them to sign loyalty oaths or (unfortunately) to "forage," i.e., take whatever food, animals or other goods they needed or wanted. Only a few units remained in one place for more than a few months.

One of these was the Third Wisconsin Cavalry, which was headquartered in Fort Scott, Kansas. Three of its companies were assigned to Vernon County in 1863 and stayed at Balltown and Deerfield almost continuously until 1865. The soldiers became so friendly with the local populace that they spent much of their time, when not patrolling, dancing and courting the local girls. Among these was Homer Pond, one of three Pond brothers who served with distinction in the regiment. Homer's brother George earned a Medal of Honor when he led a rescue of civilians Lewis and Joe Ury (Joe was a civilian scout for the regiment) against Henry Taylor's guerrillas. (Brother James Pond also won a Medal of Honor for his actions during the so-called Fort Baxter Massacre, where eighty-five cavalrymen, including many from the Third Wisconsin, were killed and mutilated by Quantrill's guerrillas while they were on their way to Texas after dodging Federal troops for two months after the raid on Lawrence.) Homer Pond did not win any medals, but he did win the hand of Lewis Ury's daughter, Barbara, in January 1865.

When General James Blunt sought to remove Captain Charles Carpenter's Company A from Balltown in the fall of 1863, the citizens wrote a petition pleading with him to let them remain to protect them from the bushwhackers' "hellish designs." They praised Carpenter and "his little band of men" for "doing all anyone could do for our safety, and the restoration of peace and quietude." Blunt apparently had second thoughts, for Company A did remain at Balltown until the end of the war. Carpenter, like Homer Pond, married a women in 1865 he met while on duty in Vernon County. His wife, Mary Elizabeth Dodge, her sisters Martha and Harriet and their cousin Sarah Emaline Garrison all married men from the Third Wisconsin Cavalry. Altogether, at least a dozen soldiers from that regiment met and married women from Vernon County.

5

Living with Soldiers and Guerrillas: Rural Missouri in 1862

For many in rural Missouri, the war began with celebrations. Troops paraded, flags were presented, florid speeches were made and men marched off to war to the sound of cheering crowds. It was the culmination of excitement that had been building during the 1860 election and especially after the election of the "Black Republican," Abraham Lincoln.

A resolution adopted at a mass meeting in Marshall in December 1860 warned that "unfriendly actions" by Northern states in refusing to enforce the Fugitive Slave Law evinced a determination to interfere with the constitutional rights of the South. Moreover, if the Republican president acted in accordance with the principles upon which he had been elected, "it will be a just cause for dissolution of the Union." At a similar meeting in Fayette, a resolution acknowledged the same grievances but cautioned that "the proper remedy is not to dissolve the union and fight against the constitution, but to stand by the union and maintain the constitution and enforcement of the laws."

One hundred women in Fayette resolved to sew a United States flag to be presented to the person who would vote to stay in the Union at the upcoming convention called by Governor Jackson to consider secession. Jane Lewis made the presentation address:

> *The time of danger is at hand. Our republic is shaken to the centre. The American union, the standard bearer in the onward march of nations, has paused in its splendid career! Our constitution, the ablest work of...mortal*

minds is decried and attacked. Our beloved country, our mighty and magnificent union, is convulsed by a moral earthquake…To man belongs the privilege of defending in the council and on the field the honor of his country, and the rights of its citizens. Woman can only weep over the woes of her native land, and pray to the Great Ruler, in whose hands are the destinies of all nations, and trust, implicitly trust, to the wise heads, the stronger arms, the braver hearts of her countrymen.

Lewis warned that—perhaps more presciently than she realized at the time—"disunion means war, civil and servile war…[and] war's tremendous horrors…outraged women, murdered children, burning homes…a desolated country…a ruined race."

But events in the summer of 1861 convinced many men and women who had hoped that war could be avoided to opt for secession instead. Although couched in terms of "resisting invasion," the celebratory events in fact meant they cast their vote for the South. James Bagwell in Macon was the first to raise South Carolina's Palmetto flag—which remained flying until Iowa troops occupied the town and tore it down. At Boonville, enthusiasts raised the Palmetto flag over the courthouse and listened to a stirring secession speech by attorney George Vest. Vest argued that the state should proclaim itself neutral until it was well armed and then cast its lot with the South. (Vest later represented Missouri in the Confederate Congress.) Local women changed their prayers from the president of the United States to praying for Jefferson Davis and the Confederacy. A committee of citizens from Boonville visited a newly arrived relative of a prominent abolitionist to inform him that "this climate would not suit him, and as they were so solicitous of his health, he left in a hurry."

The Palmetto flag was also raised at Savannah in Andrew County. In St. Joseph, the mayor and future Confederate general, M. Jeff Thompson, led a mob to the post office, climbed a ladder, tore down the United States flag and threw it in the street. He wrote later, "I had cut down the flag I once loved. I had as yet drawn no blood from its defenders, but I was now determined to strike it down wherever I found it."

In Marshall, John Marmaduke (also a future Confederate general and, after the war, Missouri governor) raised the Saline Jackson Guards. Just before he led his men to Jefferson City, the ladies of Saline County, led by Sue Isaacs, presented his men with a battle flag embroidered with the state coat of arms. Isaacs praised their valor and patriotism and their service in the "glorious cause you have so nobly espoused." Marmaduke responded in equally baroque terms, vowing "to repel the invasion of our territory and of our liberties as a state." To the women he said: "It is for you that we fight. The weakness of woman is no defense against the violence of fanaticism… [O]ur energy [will not be] abated until the barbarian emissaries of a ruthless tyrant shall be driven beyond our borders."

These were fine words, but in the event, the Saline Jackson Guards were routed in their first action at Boonville on June 17. The civilians of Boonville and Cooper County were left in the control of General Lyon and his "Dutch" soldiers. Nancy Chapman Jones, the wife of prominent merchant Caleb Jones, lost faith in the secessionist soldiers. She mentioned one who "was said to have done some of the finest running on the battle field" and who "threw away his gun and coat so as not to be encumbered in the race." She reported rumors that Governor Jackson's men had too much whiskey and too little discipline. "Jackson," she wrote, "is evidently not the man for the times." Federal troops arrested a number of residents, searched their homes and generally took what they wanted, whether they needed it or not. Jones wrote in May that she wished "some patriot ought to immortalize himself by hanging Frank Blair." It was safe to make such remarks then, but now that the Federals were in control, it could be dangerous, as Dr. George Main found out. He was arrested for treason and taken before General Lyon for having said that he wished he could have a shot at Frank Blair. Lyon let him go because mere words could not constitute treason (a relatively liberal attitude that was hardly followed universally as the war dragged on). Soldiers arrested Dr. Main again shortly afterward and brought him before Lyon a second time. Main asked for a pass so that he would not have to be "subjected to the humiliation of an arrest every half hour." Jones had nothing but scorn for the Unionists in town, such as Dr. Preston Beck—"how contemptible that fellow makes himself on all occasions."

A few days later, however, the hard hand of Federal occupation hit the Jones family. Nancy's son George was returning from searching for lost cattle when he saw some of Lyon's men marching and hurrahing Lincoln and the Union. Without thinking, George hurrahed Jeff Davis. He later said he was so angry at the "Dutch rabble" overrunning the state that he spoke before he was aware of it. A Federal captain rode up to George, pointed his pistol at him and asked if he had hurrahed Jeff Davis. George admitted he had, and two guards took him away to the Union camp at nearby Pilot Grove. When George did not show up for dinner, Nancy was frantic. Her husband laughed at her worries, but that evening, a neighbor reported that George had been marched off under armed guard. Caleb sprang into action. He ordered up his carriage and rode to the Federal encampment. Officers there denied that anyone had been arrested, but after a search, Caleb found their son. Thereafter, the incident became a family joke about George joining Frank Blair's company.

But there was little to joke about as the war continued. It became clear by the beginning of 1862, if not earlier, that the war was not going to end soon. There were no more confident assertions of the opponent's impending defeat. Guerrilla activity ramped up, and with increased Union patrols, so did searches and imprisonments. Jane Lewis was correct. War *was* bringing "tremendous horror...outraged women [and] burning homes."

The turbulent guerrilla warfare of 1862 was matched by equally turbulent political developments. Lincoln approached congressmen and senators from the border states, including Missouri, with a proposal that the Federal government would provide financial assistance if the states would begin emancipation of their slaves. It was received favorably by some of Missouri's representatives, most notably Senator John Henderson and Representative John Noell, both of whom introduced bills to accomplish that goal. But the bills were defeated, and nothing came of the effort. On April 16, President Lincoln signed a bill abolishing slavery in the District of Columbia. Writing from Boonville, Nancy Jones lamented that "the next thing will be to pass a similar one for all the border States."

On July 17, Congress passed the Second Confiscation Act, which enacted into law the same provisions of General Frémont's 1861 proclamation that were so controversial less than a year before. Section 9 provided that slaves owned by Rebels who escaped to the Union army "shall be forever free of their servitude, and not again held as slaves." Section 6 authorized the president to issue a proclamation warning that the property of all persons in rebellion was subject to being seized without compensation. And five days later, Lincoln drafted the preliminary Emancipation Proclamation, which, citing this provision, promised to free all slaves in the areas still in rebellion on January 1, 1863.

Moreover, Section 11 of the act authorized the president to enlist African Americans as soldiers in the army. None of this sat well with many Missourians, who were, after all, citizens of a loyal but slave state. Elvira Scott saw the statute as a sign of desperation. "The act will stamp infamy upon the originators of such a scheme," she wrote. "But it will not avail." She predicted that the "Negroes will fight for us [the South] as against their masters." Scott was spectacularly wrong—almost 200,000 African Americans, most of them former slaves, enlisted in the Union army. More than 8,300 African Americans from Missouri served in the army, 40 percent of the eligible males (far above the percentage of eligible white males who joined the army), and that does not count the escaped Missouri slaves who made up a large percentage of the blacks serving in Kansas units.

But the Second Confiscation Act was not the governmental action that had the most immediate effect on the guerrilla war and civilians in Missouri. That was reserved for Order No. 19 and its follow up, Order No. 24. In the summer of 1862, Confederate colonels Joseph Porter, John Poindexter and John Hughes came to central and western Missouri seeking new soldiers from what they thought was a rich pool of potential recruits dissatisfied by the Union occupation. With the Union generals in Tennessee and Arkansas demanding reinforcements and the Missouri State Militia just rounding into operational form, General John Schofield's resources were stretched thin.

John Schofield issued controversial orders requiring all loyal men to join the militia and others to register as "disloyal." *Library of Congress.*

To offset these losses, Schofield suggested to Governor Gamble that he call out additional men to serve in a state-controlled and financed militia. Gamble agreed. He directed Schofield—the commander of the Missouri State Militia ("MSM") as well as regular Federal troops in Missouri—to order into service as many men as needed. Schofield duly issued General Order No. 19 on July 22, 1862, calling for every able-bodied man to report to the nearest military post to join the Enrolled Missouri Militia ("EMM"). By the late summer of 1862, Order No. 19 had produced an additional fifty-two thousand men. Of necessity, these units were untrained and lacked even the relatively lax discipline of the full-time MSM. A distressing number of men took advantage of their newfound military authority to harass, or even rob or kill, neighbors against whom they bore grudges or whom they suspected or knew to be Southern sympathizers.

Some Union men were troubled by Order No. 19 because it was, in effect, conscription even before the Federal government began conscription and a practice that had previously been prohibited. Governor Gamble and General Schofield did not consult higher authorities before taking this drastic step. The latter informed Washington that he suggested the measure to Gamble and ordered it into effect because the level of guerrilla violence reached the point that it was an "immediate and pressing necessity…to call at once all of the militia of the State" into service. It would have the additional ultimate benefit of allowing Schofield to release regular volunteer units for service in other theaters, such as with General Grant, who repeatedly called for more troops.

But the most controversial provision of the decree was its clarifying Order No. 24, which provided that *disloyal* men report to the nearest military post to register as such. They were to surrender their arms return to their homes and businesses, where—supposedly—they would not be disturbed if they "continue[d] quietly attending to their ordinary and legitimate business and in no way [gave] aid or comfort to the enemy." Some Federal commanders anticipated, correctly, that having to register as "disloyal" would "create a stampede of secesh" to Southern arms that would bolster the forces then being gathered by recruiters such as Porter and Poindexter. And, indeed, Union soldiers distributing the order reported that the countryside was "greatly excited" about the order, and "a considerable number left their homes with intention to again in some way resist its execution." In Southwest Missouri, Rachel Anderson confided to her diary that "secesh move off in a silent procession by the light of the moon leaving their families in the midst of their enemies."

Southern sympathizers like Caleb Jones and John Scott were too old to have to make the choice between joining the EMM or declaring themselves disloyal. But those of military age—eighteen to forty-five—were not so lucky. Men who thought they could keep a low profile and remain neutral were going to have to declare themselves one way or another. In a civil war, neutrality was no longer an option.

Willard Mendenhall of Lexington was one such man. Before the war, Mendenhall owned a company that made carriages. His building was taken over by Federal troops for use as a commissary. Although he professed that he loved the Union *and* preferred to live in a slave state, he soon came to the conclusion (as nearly all Southern sympathizers did) that this was a war against slavery. Nevertheless, he chose not to join either the Confederate army or the EMM. Mendenhall believed his first loyalty was to his family, and he decided to stay home for their protection. His decision to register as disloyal brought him little sympathy from the local EMM commander, Colonel Henry Neal. When Mendenhall complained about soldiers seizing his family's food, Neal replied, "Go to Jeff Davis for protection." The remark was especially cutting because Mendenhall and Neal had been friends and fellow Masons before the war. Friendship now meant little.

John Brannock was attending college in Fayette at the outbreak of the war. He returned to his wife, Lizzie, and their two small children that summer. Their home was attacked by Jennison's men, who, although the Brannocks said they were pro-Union, took nearly everything they had, sparing only their house. John was arrested, but a former classmate was an officer of the regiment and let him go. John tried to farm a family member's place in Cass County, but Kansas troops destroyed that as well. Finally, when Order No. 19 was handed down, John decided to join "the army which he conceived to be the *right* one rather than go into the militia." He believed that the order required him to choose one side or the other—trying to sit it out as Mendenhall did was not going to work for him. John and his brother Thomas managed to join a regiment in Shelby's Missouri brigade. Presumably because of his education, John was appointed a corporal. He and his brother returned to central Missouri when Shelby led a raid from the Arkansas border to the Missouri River in October 1863. Thomas was wounded at the Battle of Marshall on October 13. John stayed behind to take care of his brother. Lizzie managed to see them at the hospital in Marshall before both were shipped off to the Gratiot Street Prison in St. Louis and later to the prison in Alton, Illinois. John and Thomas remained as prisoners of war until they were paroled in March 1865. Thus, Lizzie had to face more than two years of the war alone with their two small children.

Many women were left at home to face the uncertainties of war without their husbands, sons or fathers. More than 109,000 men from Missouri served in the Union army. About 40,000 Missourians joined the Confederate army. These numbers do not include 14,000 men who were in the Missouri State Militia for three years or the estimated 52,000 men who complied with orders to join the Enrolled Missouri Militia and served for varying periods ranging from a few days to a few months.

There is no firm estimate of the number of men who "went to the brush" and became guerrillas. Contemporary reports suggest that as many as four to five hundred guerrillas under various leaders gathered for the raid on Lawrence, Kansas, in August 1863, and a similar number participated in the Battle of Centralia, Missouri, in September 1864. The fluidity of guerrilla membership and lack of records makes it impossible to be any more precise. Although the exact number of active guerrillas operating in Missouri at any one time cannot be determined, the nature of their tactics—ambush, hit-and-run and surprise raids on towns—was such that a small number could cause a great deal of disruption.

"Formation of Guerrilla Bands," by Adalbert John Volck, from V. Blada, *Sketches from the Civil War in North America, 1861, '62, '63. Library of Congress.*

With so many men gone, it was left to many women to assume new roles. In addition to normal prewar household duties, women now had to keep the farm running, to supervise the slaves, to protect their families. Although women were denied a political role—they could not vote, for example—they nonetheless expressed political views. And that could lead to trouble.

Elvira Scott was the fifty-year-old wife of John Scott, a successful merchant in Miami, Saline County. Miami was an important port for the shipment of hemp before the war. But after the war began, life in Miami was more a matter of survival than buying or selling. Elvira Scott was an excellent musician and amateur painter. She was also a strong secessionist with a virulent anti-German and anti-Irish bias. She kept a diary that provides one of the few contemporary day-to-day records of life in rural Missouri during the war.

Scott confided her strong views to her diary. She wrote, for example, in March 1862 that Miami was full of refugees from Jackson County who were not "active Secessionists," but it was enough that they were "men of property, who sympathized with the Southern cause & owned Negroes." By contrast, the Union soldiers in town were "Dutch & Irish laborers who have nothing at stake." Better folk—people like her—were "kept under subjection by the lowest most unprincipled Dutch, with very few American hirelings."

Scott's disdain for the Union militia is evident from her diary and the contrast she drew between the Federal troops and the guerrillas who visited Miami. The former were ignorant, lazy, filthy and the "lowest, most desperate looking specimens of humanity it has ever been my lot to witness." Guerrillas, on the other hand, she described as well-dressed in "picturesque style," clean, polite, good-looking, intelligent, "refined & courteous in their manner, their language correct & gentlemanly." Where the motives she attributed to Union soldiers were the mere desire to plunder and terrorize their betters because they had the power to do so, she admired the guerrillas for their "reckless daring," "ready to sell their lives as dearly as possible," driven to extreme violence only by the dangers that surrounded anyone who dared to defy the Federal government.

There might be more than mere partisan sentiment to Scott's comments. Recent research by historians such as Mark Geiger and Don Bowen suggests that many members of the guerrilla bands (or at least of those who can be identified) came from relatively wealthy slave-owning families. The families were among the strongest supporters of secession, even going to the extent of mortgaging their land to pay for equipping such units as the Saline Jackson Guards and Shelby's regiment. That someone like Elvira

Scott, herself a member of the merchant and slaveholding elite of central Missouri, would find these men far more admirable than "foreigners" who spoke poor English is not surprising. Moreover, most of the Union soldiers Scott encountered were farmers or workingmen—she was scandalized to find out that the major commanding at Marshall was a *blacksmith!*

On March 11, a company of Missouri State Militia led by Captain Peter Ostermeyer rode into town—"Federals at last." They arrested several men and moved on. But on April 26, more soldiers appeared, and this time they arrested John Scott. Authorities held him for a week but released him on parole and the posting of a $3,000 bond to guarantee his good behavior.

In recounting John's experience, Scott wrote: "Gentlemen of the highest social &—a year ago—political position are hunted down and shot like dogs if they do not come forward & take the oath to support these usurpations." Scott raged in her diary against the provisional state government that "arrogated to itself supreme power." She lamented that thousands of the best men were in the South fighting for their "inalienable rights, life, liberty & the pursuit of happiness" (note that Scott, like many Southern sympathizers of the time, left out that part of the Declaration of Independence about "all

"Searching for arms," by Adalbert John Volck, from V. Blada, *Sketches from the Civil War in North America, 1861, '62, '63. Library of Congress.*

men are created equal"). She believed that the "national airs" sung by the Federal soldiers were not just insincere but also beyond their comprehension. They were, she was convinced, in it strictly for the money and plunder that their position gave them license to take with impunity.

Scott's low opinion of the state and federal government, however, landed her in trouble. In early July, a soldier handed her a document from the local commander, Lieutenant Adam Bax, that she thought was intended for her husband until she saw her name on it. "The time has passed," it read, "when treasonable language goes unpunished. A Ladies place is to fulfill household duties, and not to spread treason and excite men to rebellion." She was ordered to report personally to military headquarters until such time as the commanding officer is "fully convinced that you behave yourself as a Lady Ought." Scott was "*indignant, outraged*" that such an "ignorant, degraded class of men" would instruct her on the proper duties of a *lady*. She had never—at least publicly—uttered any treasonable sentiments, whatever she thought privately. (It apparently did not occur to Scott that private conversations in her house might be reported to Federal authorities by her slaves.)

John was incensed as well, but when a man criticized the Union soldiers, he could find himself in serious trouble. John unburdened himself to a fellow merchant. This man, whom Elvira characterized as a former "violent & uncompromising secessionist" but now a "pusillanimous sycophant," reported John's remarks to Lieutenant Bax. He told the lieutenant that John had called him a "contemptible puppy" and a "low-lived scoundrel." No doubt John had used those very words, but (according to Elvira) John had said that the officer would qualify for such scorn only *if* (her emphasis) he had charged her out of spite or revenge.

Elvira found John held at gunpoint by a squad of soldiers. Lieutenant Bax approached her armed with three revolvers. "Madam, you shall not insult the flag of my country," he said. Scott shot back, "I have insulted no flag but I have neither country nor flag to protect me." Soldiers led John away to their camp at the fairground. Elvira went home, expecting to hear that her husband had been shot. He was released on parole with orders to report to Marshall for trial.

Later, Elvira led a delegation of ladies to meet Lieutenant Bax to discuss the charges against them. The charges were petty: their children called the soldiers abolitionists (Bax had to agree that many of them were); some had hurrahed Jeff Davis (the soldiers had egged them on); and another had "talked in her garden," presumably disparaging the Union cause. They all denied making political remarks or defended their children as too small to

"Jemison's [*sic*] Jayhawkers," by Adalbert John Volck, from *Blada's War Sketches. Library of Congress.*

realize what they were saying. The lieutenant did not say who the informants might be. (Again, none seem to have considered that their black servants might have told the soldiers what they had heard.) Scott proceeded to dress Bax down, pointing out that Jennison's Jayhawkers had stolen a large number of slaves, and as far as Bax's boast that the rebellion would be crushed, she proudly noted that Southern arms had been victorious that summer before Richmond. Scott dismissed his threats. She was not afraid of him and said that she did not come from a cowardly race—*her* ancestors had fought Indians in the wilderness and were native Americans for centuries. This last jab was intended to disparage Bax's nativity, but he was too dense to realize it (or just ignored it). Bax undoubtedly was eager to end the meeting because, according to Scott, he unexpectedly found "ladies to deal with who would not condescend to be abusive, but yet did not fear him in the least. He was hardly prepared, I think, for such womanly dignity & fearlessness. He thought, I suppose, that we would come, frightened & trembling, begging his mercy."

John was held at Marshall a week, but he was acquitted in the end. Scott wrote that her husband had also bawled out Lieutenant Bax for his disrespectful language. The "little lieutenant" became frightened of the consequences if his superiors found out, and he begged the Scotts' forgiveness. Thus, the incident closed.

The Scotts, especially John, were lucky. Both Union soldiers and guerrillas generally refrained from physical abuse of white women, and so Elvira's tirades were bold but far less likely to result in punishment than John's complaints. Men, on the other hand, were frequently jailed or even shot for making the kind of statements he made about Bax. And being called before the authorities by a disgruntled neighbor was hardly unusual.

6

RELIGION AND RELIGIOUS FREEDOM IN THE MIDST OF GUERRILLA WAR

A s she sat in the St. Charles Presbyterian Church, Mary Easton Sibley became agitated and then angry. Sibley was not raised to be particularly religious, but in mid-life she joined the Old School Presbyterian Church. Now, Pastor Robert Farris—her pastor—was not only talking politics in the pulpit, but he was also talking secession. It was July 1861. The state was in turmoil. Nathaniel Lyon had captured Camp Jackson in May, Union and Missouri State Guard troops clashed at Boonville in June and there were reports of men burning bridges and shooting into trains.

Federal troops under General John Pope had camped at St. Charles. And now Farris offered a prayer that "the State of Missouri might have the power granted to it by the Almighty '*to drive out the invaders*,'" an obvious reference to Pope's Union soldiers. He further prayed that "they might be made strong to resist oppression." Moreover, Farris had publicly declared that he was a "revolutionist." Sibley wrote an indignant letter to the provost marshal in St. Louis demanding that Farris be dealt with.

It took over a year, but in September 1862, staunch Unionist Franklin Dick, now provost marshal, arrested Farris and put him in the Gratiot Street Prison. Dick concluded Farris was disloyal and gave him six weeks to get out of town and the state. Farris used the time to good advantage and proved that, if one has powerful local enemies, one should have even more powerful national friends.

Farris wrote to United States Supreme Court justice David Davis, a close friend of Lincoln's, seeking help. Alerted to Farris's maneuver, Dick wrote the president directly, arguing that "Farris is one of the most impudent, persist[ent] and ingenious Rebels in the State, and as a Minister, has wielded a powerful influence in aid of the rebellion." Lincoln nevertheless decided that Farris could return to Missouri. Dick refused to allow Farris back in the state. The minister once again appealed to Justice Davis, and once again the president ordered Dick to allow Farris to return. This time Dick complied, presumably grudgingly. Sibley's reaction to these events is not recorded.

Missourians took their religion seriously. Although in many ways a frontier society with its attendant rough edges, by 1860 there were 1,579 churches in Missouri. Presbyterians such as Sibley's church accounted for 215 of them, but the majority were either Methodist Episcopal South (526) or Southern Baptist (458). The word "South" in the names was significant, for it reflected a division of previously united churches over slavery.

The tradition of what Marcus McArthur calls "apolitical theology" had deep roots in Missouri: the church had a strictly spiritual jurisdiction, and ministers should not become involved in political issues. But in the 1840s, church unity began to crack. Northern ministers agitated for the church to take a stand on the slavery issue. The matter came to a head in the Methodist Church in 1844. Bishop James Andrew of Georgia inherited slaves, and his wife owned slaves. Northern Methodists demanded that he free the slaves, but Georgia law prohibited it. After an impassioned debate, the Methodist Conference voted to suspend Andrew from office while he owned slaves. Missouri's Methodists joined their Southern brethren in voting against suspension. Southern delegates organized the Methodist Church South in 1845, and Missouri's conference voted to join that group. By 1859, the Methodist Church South had 44,000 members in Missouri and the Methodist Church North only 6,000.

The Baptists split along geographical lines in the slavery debate as well. The Southern Baptist Association, whose members had sought unsuccessfully to have the church endorse a policy allowing slaveholders to be missionaries, was organized in 1845. Missouri's General Convention joined the following year.

The Presbyterians had separated in the 1830s over other doctrinal questions into Old School and New School churches. Old School Presbyterians, such as Sibley, generally sought to avoid the slavery question altogether while New School Presbyterians—like the Northern factions of the Methodists and Baptists—supported antislavery political positions.

Although there were only two Unitarian churches in Missouri at the outbreak of the war, Unitarian minister William Greenleaf Eliot was the most prominent cleric in the state. He was not only a well-known religious figure but also a founder of Washington University in St. Louis and a leader in a number of other civic activities. He also exemplified the "political" preacher who used his pulpit to promote the Union cause. Where apolitical ministers justified noninterference in political affairs based on the passage in Matthew 2:21—"Render therefore unto Caesar the things that are Caesar's, and unto God the things that are God's"—Eliot's take was precisely the opposite. Eliot argued that "no one who loves his country, or has any interest in its welfare, can or ought to be silent." Neutrality was, in effect, a stance in favor of rebellion, for it was "a Christian duty to defend our country from invasion and rebellion, peaceably if we can, forcibly if we must."

A staunch Unionist preaching in St. Louis, a city filled with Federal troops, could make such overtly political statements from the pulpit without fear. But for ministers in the countryside life was not so simple. A Northern Methodist minister in Shelbyville was threatened with a coat of tar and feathers for supporting the Union. A Baptist minister, Bartlett Anderson of Randolph County, was accused of preaching "treasonable and disloyal sentiments," a charge he vehemently denied. He said that he never introduced politics in the pulpit and was "opposed to the preaching of politics from the pulpit or otherwise using the pulpit than for purely religious purposes." Anderson's protests were of no avail. He was sent to St. Louis for trial before a military commission. The commission acquitted him and ordered his release. Anderson returned home on December 8. On December 24, 1862, General Samuel Curtis issued General Order No. 35, which authorized provost marshals and commanders to arrest "notoriously bad and dangerous men," even without proof of any wrongdoing, and to require them to post a bond for good behavior or to imprison or banish them. General Lewis Merrill, the commander of the district that included Randolph County, was obviously dissatisfied with Anderson's release. He immediately ordered Anderson banished to some point "east of the State of Illinois and north of Indianapolis, Indiana." Anderson apparently did not comply with the order right away and was charged in March 1863 with having made numerous statements in support of the Confederacy. The authorities sent him before another military commission. What happened next is unclear (perhaps he was found guilty but paroled), but in any event, Anderson was allowed to remain in St. Louis.

Robert Farris ran afoul of the authorities for public prayers opposing Union forces, but ministers did not have to go that far in more sensitive areas. Lexington was a hotbed of secession sentiment and sent many men to the

Samuel McPheeters was the center of a controversy over whether ministers had to preach sermons in favor of the Union. From John Grasty, *Memoir of Rev. Samuel B. McPheeters*, 1871.

Confederate army and guerrilla bands. As late as 1865, when Northern victory was ensured, Southern Methodist minister W.B. McFarland was removed from the pulpit merely for failing to lead his congregation in special prayers of thanksgiving for recent Northern military victories.

The most well-known case of military interference with religious affairs involved Old School Presbyterian minister Samuel McPheeters of the Pine Street Presbyterian Church in St. Louis. Unlike Robert Farris, who publicly made his political views known, McPheeters refrained from any such comments from the pulpit on the basis that the "Church…owes its allegiance only to Jesus Christ."

But in the tense atmosphere of St. Louis in the summer of 1862, when Federal forces were suffering defeats, guerrillas were terrorizing Unionists in the countryside and Confederate officers were roaming North Missouri recruiting hundreds of men, neutrality was seen by ardent Unionists as endorsement of the rebellion. And then, on Sunday, June 8, Samuel Robbins and his wife brought their newborn son to the Pine Street Church to be baptized before a congregation that included such staunch Unionists as attorney George Strong. When asked what name the family chose, they responded "*Sterling Price* Robbins," no doubt to the gasps of many of the faithful. Later, McPheeters claimed that when he was first told that was to be the child's name, he thought it "a jest," and he was just as surprised as anyone else when he learned that Robbins was serious. Believing, as he later told President Lincoln, that he had no choice, he proceeded with the ceremony. Thus began another prolonged Missouri dispute that could only be ended by the president himself.

On June 18, Strong and twenty-nine other church members wrote to McPheeters, charging that the baptism of Sterling Price Robbins was "a premeditated insult to the government and all its friends in the Pine Street Church…a public and sacrilegious prostitution of a sacred ordinance of God's house, to the gratification…of the most contemptible and malicious feelings of hostility to 'the powers that be.'"

In December 1862, both sides of the controversy published letters setting forth their positions. On December 19, the government took action. Provost Marshal Dick ordered McPheeters and his wife banished. Dick's justification for the order (issued without even a hearing before a military commission) was that McPheeters "refuses to declare whether he is in favor of the success of the authorities of the nation in their efforts to put down a cruel and desolating rebellion." Dick also ordered that the Pine Street Church and its records be turned over to a committee of its members headed by George Strong.

Following the principle that persons with powerful local enemies need powerful national friends, McPheeters sought the help of Attorney General Edward Bates, a family friend and fellow Presbyterian. McPheeters traveled to Washington, where Bates accompanied him to a personal interview with the president on December 27. Lincoln listened as McPheeters read a prepared statement. The president asked about the "most singular baptism." Bates pointed out that McPheeters followed church law in baptizing the child with the parents' chosen name, and he further noted the extraordinary nature of the provision in Dick's order whereby the military was seizing a church, not for a hospital, but for a church where the military would prescribe the content of the sermons.

Lincoln was noncommittal at the meeting but ended up sending an order to the commander of the department, General Samuel Curtis, directing that the banishment order be lifted. Curtis and Dick protested, but Lincoln noted that there was no actual evidence against McPheeters, just a "suspicion of his secret sympathies." He cautioned "that the U.S. government must not, as by this order, undertake to run the churches." Military authorities could deal with anyone who posed a danger to the "public interest," Lincoln wrote, "but let the churches as such, take care of themselves. It will not do for the U.S. to appoint Trustees, Supervisors, or other agents for the churches."

As far as Lincoln was concerned, the matter was done. But Union authorities in Missouri were not going to let a mere presidential directive stop them from suppressing what they conceived as Confederate sentiment. Although Lincoln disapproved of the takeover of the Pine Street Church, Dick left Strong's committee in charge until March. Moreover, McPheeters still could not preach in Missouri. He attempted to resign, but his congregation asked him to remain. In late 1863, more than three dozen of McPheeters's supporters sent letters and a petition asking the president to allow the deposed minister to resume his duties.

The president was puzzled and offended by the notion that he was somehow responsible for McPheeters's continued predicament. Lincoln observed that one of the letter writers said, "Is it not a strange illustration of the condition of things that the question of who shall be allowed to preach in a church in St. Louis shall be decided by the *President* of *the United States?*" The president was probably thinking the same thing. He denied depriving McPheeters of "any ecclesiastical right, or authorized, or excused its being done by any one deriving authority from me...The assumption that I am keeping Dr. M. from preaching in his church is monstrous. If any one is doing this, by pretense of my authority, I will thank any one who can, to make out and present me, a specific case against him. If, after all, the Dr. is kept out by the majority of his own parishioners, and my official power is sought to force him in over their heads, I decline that also." McPheeters returned to the pulpit in January 1864. One year later, he moved to Mulberry, Kentucky. McPheeters died in 1870.

And Samuel Robbins? He was tried by a military commission at the insistence of, among others, George Strong and banished for the temerity of naming his son after the Confederate general. After the war, Robbins returned to St. Louis. By 1888, Sterling Price Robbins was an officer of the St. Louis Vise & Tool Company.

The treatment of McPheeters and others discouraged many ministers from taking churches. And those who attempted to remain as neutral as McPheeters could run into similar troubles. For example, as part of its strictures on those who could hold certain offices, the state legislature required ministers to take loyalty oaths to be able to conduct lawful marriages. Apparently the law was not as rigorously enforced as it might have been, for in 1864, the legislature passed another law legitimizing any marriages performed by clergy who had failed to take the oath.

All of these political maneuvers engrossed the elite, but ordinary Missourians went to church to seek solace and hope. As one member of the Pine Street Church told Reverend McPheeters, "We have the war all the week, and want the gospel on Sunday." Diaries and letters of the period are filled with fervent prayers. At first, many of Southern sympathies prayed for the success of the rebellion or repulse of the Union "invaders." Soon the nature of the prayers shifted to ones for the safety of their loved ones, whether in the military, guerrillas or those who stayed home to chance the dangers of the guerrilla war from both sides. By 1863, the prayers were for the end of the war. No doubt, those of Northern sympathies felt the same.

7

FEMALE COURIERS, FEMALE SOLDIERS AND CHILDREN FIGHT THE WAR

Letters to and from home were an important part of keeping up morale in both places. The volume of mail handled during the Civil War mushroomed into an estimated 180,000 letters per day. Soldiers on both sides eagerly awaited news from home. Loved ones eagerly—and sometimes apprehensively—awaited news from their husbands, sons and fathers.

Exchanging letters with Missouri's Union troops was relatively easy compared to sending and receiving letters in the Confederate army. George Wolz, a private in the Missouri State Militia, wrote to his family back in Grundy County regularly from his stations in Southwest and Central Missouri. Wolz's letters, like those of many soldiers, frequently began with a comment about the dates of the letters received from home and ended with the request to send more letters more often. He described some firefights he was in but mostly wrote about the routine matters of camp—fruit the men had found to eat, dancing with the local girls, where they were camped and (ever the farmer's son) the nature and quality of the crops grown in the area. Almost all of them assured his parents, brother and sister of his good health. And he often passed along news of other men in his regiment to be given to their families.

The mail from the front was not only shared with family and neighbors but also published in the local newspapers. For example, the Wisconsin papers published letters and articles about the doings of the Third Wisconsin Cavalry stationed in Missouri and Kansas for nearly the entire war. And if the worst happened, a bundle of letters from the deceased family member became a treasure to be read and shared again and again.

Back home in Wolz's hometown of Trenton, the residents anxiously awaited the tri-weekly hack from Chillicothe bringing letters and news of the war and loved ones. Its arrival was "the signal for a crowd to gather and listen while the address on each letter and paper was called out by the worthy postmistress, Mrs. Collier." The gathering then "adjourned to some convenient fence corner to hear the news about the war" read aloud by Mr. A.K. Sykes. The family's letters to Wolz, which unfortunately were not preserved but whose content can be inferred from his replies, provided news of the neighborhood, who was sick, how the crops were doing and the family's comings and goings.

Communications between men serving in the Confederate army and their families back home in Missouri was far more complicated than merely addressing a letter and mailing it. News of families in the Confederate states or relatives in the Confederate armies was sporadic and often delayed. Rachel Anderson, for example, found out only on September 1, 1864, that her brother John had been killed at Antietam almost two years earlier.

Moreover, correspondence with anyone in the rebellious states was prohibited. A person caught in Missouri sending, or receiving, a letter to a Confederate soldier was subject to being tried by a military commission and jailed or banished.

In military courts-martial, the charging documents identified the Article of War the soldier was accused of violating. The charging documents in military commissions were more vague. They said little more than that the correspondent had violated the "laws of war," without identifying which law of war or where such a law could be found. Simply corresponding with the enemy, even one's own son or brother, was considered contrary to the laws of war. Sometimes the charges were couched in terms of "giving aid, comfort and encouragement" to the enemy—an echo of the definition of treason in the United States Constitution.

But family bonds were too strong to be deterred by legal prohibitions or threatened penalties. A few intrepid women were not going to let Union soldiers prevent them, their families or their friends from seeking and providing news to their kinfolk in the Southern armies. They sent and received letters by couriers who slipped between lines, some men and others women—even Catholic nuns.

In 1863, Union soldiers burst into the home of Mary Cleveland. In searching the place, they found letters from her brother Charles, then serving with General Price in Mississippi, letters she and her mother had written to him but had not yet sent and letters from neighbors to their kin. Perhaps she could have talked her way out of serious trouble, but she had angry words with a Union captain. The local provost marshal sent Cleveland to St. Louis for trial on charges of corresponding with and helping others correspond with Confederate soldiers.

At trial, she declined to answer when questioned about the author of the letters in her possession—even though a comparison of some of the letters with ones she admitted writing showed "without doubt" that they were in her hand. Cleveland claimed not even to know who the authors of the other letters were. She had to admit that she received a letter from her brother—it was addressed to "My Dear Sister."

When pressed to swear that she knew nothing, Cleveland would only "affirm" the truth of her answers because she would not take any oath that involved the Almighty. Whether she feared divine retribution or simply perjury is not known. In any event, her testimony was received with extreme skepticism. A note in her file from one of those in attendance says that he had never seen a person "more willful & deceptive" and that Cleveland was a "veritable 'she-adder.'" Cleveland was found guilty and sentenced to banishment beyond Union lines, despite her pleas for mitigation because her elderly mother was "melancholy" and "deranged."

Postwar reminiscences confirm Cleveland's guilt. Virginia Yates McCanne recalled that when the Union soldiers came to search the house, Cleveland stalled them while she burned most of the incriminating documents in the kitchen fireplace. The letters had been delivered by a "little old French woman" (one of Cleveland's letters said it was a nun from the Sisters of Charity) who had them sewn into her petticoat.

Banishment was a common sentence for women. Cleveland was among forty men and women sent to Mississippi in May 1863. The *New York Times* wrote approvingly of the punishment, saying that these persons "are rebels in the gravest and grossest sense of the word…The South is the proper place for them."

James Bagwell was a wealthy man who lived in Woodville, just a few miles southeast of Hudson in Randolph County. He was notorious for having been the first person to raise a Rebel flag after Fort Sumter was fired on. Bagwell managed to keep himself out of serious misfortune for the next two years. But in early 1863, he let slip to his clerk, a Union informant, that "his women folk were writing letters and he feared they would get him in trouble."

Bagwell's wife and daughter, Augusta and Zaidee, were then living in a St. Louis hotel. Apparently, based on either Bagwell's slip of the tongue or a tip from the women's black servant, the authorities in St. Louis raided their room. There they found twenty-eight letters for Confederate soldiers from various families and a love letter from Zaidee to her beau, William F. Luckett, a lieutenant in the Confederate army serving near Vicksburg. Both were charged with violating the laws of war by writing to, or assisting others in writing to, the enemy and with encouraging the enemy by such letters.

Augusta testified that she wrote a letter to J.M. Flannigan, an officer in Price's army, in response to a letter she had received from him. She would only say that she got Flannigan's letter from an "Irish woman whose name I do not know" and gave her reply to "a boy to be sent…I gave him no directions. I do not know in whose employ the boy was." She "declined to answer" any questions about the letters she received for forwarding to others. The commission had little difficulty in convicting her of the offenses charged.

Zaidee's crime was in writing to her lover in the army and sending him a pair of gloves and a photograph. The letter was mostly gossip about events and acquaintances. Presumably the most damning portions giving aid, comfort and encouragement read: "We…hope you will give the Feds your best Minnie ball, and shoot a few extra balls in revenge for us. You may look for several kisses in this letter, and you will find them. Write soon to your true and devoted rebel, ZAIDEE J. BAGWELL."

As permitted by commission procedures, Zaidee was allowed to submit a brief, apparently drafted by her lawyer (whose name does not appear in the available records). She first argued for mercy because, as a young and inexperienced girl who was just writing to her sweetheart, she was completely unaware that it might violate any law.

As a legal basis for dismissal, Zaidee raised two arguments—one very unusual and one strikingly modern, but both ultimately losers. First, Zaidee claimed that the commission lacked jurisdiction because the Fifth Amendment to the Constitution provides that citizens who are not in the armed forces (and thus not subject to military law) can be charged only by an indictment handed down by a grand jury. Even if the declaration of martial law and the suspension of habeas corpus allowed citizens to be tried by military tribunals, the orders establishing commissions provided that they could only try cases not triable by courts-martial. Because violations of the laws of war are triable by courts-martial, Zaidee asserted the commission lacked the power to try her. The notion that civilians were entitled to a court-martial was even more radical than that the military could try them by a commission, although practically speaking, there was little difference between the two procedures.

But Zaidee's second argument would, if made today, have special force. The only evidence against her came from her own testimony. She contended that her inculpatory statements should not have been admitted into evidence because she had not been warned that they could be used against her at trial. "Think you," she wrote, "if advised of my rights, if properly admonished and warned of the humble responsibility I was assuming, I should have made any statement that could have been employed against me!" The commission found none of her legal arguments persuasive and convicted Zaidee as well.

Both Augusta and Zaidee were sentenced to banishment to the South (or perhaps Canada, the documents indicate both as destinations). At James Bagwell's request, General Schofield mitigated the punishment to parole. Perhaps he was influenced by Bagwell's wealth, for he was required to post a $10,000 bond for his wife and $5,000 bond for his daughter. They remained in St. Louis for a few weeks. As a condition of their parole, Augusta and Zaidee had to report periodically in writing to the provost marshal. Both were given permission to return home to Woodville, but the periodic reports were still required. Their convictions did not subdue the women's attitudes. In July 1863, Augusta reported that she "has the *honor* to report herself, as yet, no subjugated rebel." This earned a note from the provost marshal declaring, "This should be shown to the general," but apparently no punishment was forthcoming for her impertinence.

Some women took an even more active role in supporting the rebellion. In mid-1862, Maggie Creath and Lizzie Powell were suspected of having smuggled fifty thousand percussion caps out of Hannibal in their petticoats and given them to guerrillas. Creath "made quite a sensation" when she appeared with a guerrilla named Clay Price in Monroe County, decked out in Rebel colors and with "a brace of pistols ornamenting her taper waist." The local commander noted that the two women's "beauty, talents and superior education have made many a man a bushwhacker who except for their influence would have been an honest man."

Lizzie Powell was a nineteen-year-old woman described by fascinated Union men as "young, beautiful & accomplished." In the summer of 1862, she openly discouraged young men from complying with Order No. 19 to join the Enrolled Missouri Militia, telling them that doing so would be an "everlasting disgrace." She was also accused of attending parties in "rebel colors," a claim she confirmed in her diary.

On September 29, 1862, Captain William Poillon came to her home to arrest her. Poillon was a hard-bitten veteran of the Mexican War and a staunch Union man whose duties as a civilian scout for the army in Audrain County included "ferreting out treason."

To make the arrest, Poillon brought with him not only an unusually large force—forty to fifty soldiers—but also a number of officers who were eager to meet this notorious and attractive Rebel. When Poillon began to introduce his companions, Powell "requested him to dispense with this, as it was not my desire to be introduced to those whose acquaintance I had not sought and did not expect to cultivate." She was taken before General Merrill, the district commander. After some verbal sparring about the rebellion, the general remarked "that he had never met an intelligent southern lady in Missouri. I replied that he had been very unfortunate in his associations." He forwarded his "fascinating captive" on to Palmyra to face punishment. Powell's escort was Lieutenant William Easley, who, like the other Federal officers, was smitten by her. Easley offered to help her escape to Illinois, but she refused to go.

At Palmyra, she was brought before William Strachan, a provost marshal who became notorious for sparing a Confederate soldier from execution when his wife acceded to his demand for sexual favors while her child waited outside his office. Strachan was "a low, red-faced man, with small, keen black eyes and dark hair, brown whiskers and heavy mustache." After a "spirited discussion of her circumstances," Strachan sent her to be confined at a local hotel with her friend Maggie Creath. The authorities decided that they would banish Powell and Creath.

Powell became seriously ill, possibly with tuberculosis, and requested a leave of absence to be served in Hannibal. General John McNeil, who earned his own notoriety by ordering the execution of ten Confederate soldiers in retaliation for the murder of a Union informer, met her on December 10. He said he would let her go completely free if she signed a loyalty oath, but Powell refused. McNeil profusely complimented her and expressed his admiration for her spirit and—referring to the recent executions—said she must think him inhuman and barbarous. "I frankly replied that I did," Powell answered.

Powell remained more or less free in Hannibal. On New Year's Day, she met none other than Zaidee Bagwell, who was traveling to St. Louis. A Union citizen, William Newland, complained that Powell was allowed free run of the town. He noted that she was completely defiant of the Union soldiers, "but about one half of them are in love with her." The new provost marshal, T.D. Price, came to see her. She wrote in her diary that he "solicits an introduction and passes several compliments; [I] refuse for [the] reason that I do not wish to devote the evening to entertaining a Federal officer." Price was befuddled. He finally wrote to the provost marshal general in St. Louis urging that she not be sent north but banished to Dixie. He pointed out that when Powell was served with the original banishment order, she simply refused to go—and the authorities did not know what to do about it. In a postscript, Price (like the other Federal officers) described her as a "young and withal quite fascinating 'King-Bee' among the 'Secesh.'" Partly because of her ill health and partly because they did not seem to know how to handle her defiance, the Federal authorities released her unconditionally in February 1863. Margaret Creath signed a bond for good behavior and was released as well.

Union women in Missouri did not have to conceal their support and contributions to the war effort. Some went beyond merely rolling bandages or writing letters for wounded soldiers. They joined the army itself. Of the three million soldiers who served in the military during the war, a small but significant number were women. No one knows the exact number, but it was likely in the hundreds.

The best-known female soldier serving in a Missouri regiment was Frances Clayton (sometimes also rendered as Clalin or Clatin). Although she and her husband (whose name was said to be Elmer) lived in Minnesota before the war, they joined a Missouri regiment in 1861. Clayton's story was featured in several newspapers in 1863 after she left the service. She recounted in interviews that her regiment fought at Fort Donelson, where she was wounded slightly. She fought beside her husband at the Battle of Stones River in

Frances Clayton, shown here in uniform, was one of several hundred women who, disguised as men, served in the army. *Library of Congress.*

December 1862, when he was killed. Clayton recalled that when ordered to fix bayonets and charge, she stepped over his body to continue the fight. She was discharged in early 1863. Clayton was described as a "very tall, masculine looking woman bronzed by exposure" who smoked, drank and gambled like a man. Her photographs in uniform and in a dress were widely circulated.

Unfortunately, the circumstances of her service are vague and unverifiable. She may have enlisted under the name of "Jack Williams." None of the meager details of soldiers with the last name of Williams in any of the Missouri units at either battle match the details of her or her husband's service as recounted in the newspapers. It appears that, if they joined a Missouri regiment, both Frances and her husband enlisted under assumed names. A John Williams enlisted in Company H, Seventeenth Missouri Infantry, in 1861 but was discharged shortly thereafter because he "[p]roved to be a woman."

The Library of Congress identifies Clayton's unit as the Fourth Missouri Heavy Artillery and Company I, Thirteenth Missouri Cavalry, based on a handwritten notation on the back of her photograph in uniform. The photograph was taken by Samuel Masury, a Boston photographer, most likely in connection with an 1865 lecture tour. The flyer for the lecture says that Clayton would appear in "cavalry rig and go through with the sword exercise." She concluded her show by appearing "in woman's attire." Her pictures—no doubt the Masury photographs—were offered for sale.

One Masury photograph shows her hat with crossed sabers and what appears to be the number "thirteen," which may account for attributing her service to the Thirteenth Missouri Cavalry. However, these were likely props for her lecture to illustrate the point that she could pass for a man while in uniform. The first unit did not exist, and the second was not organized until September 1864; its members were veterans recruited from the Missouri State Militia. A "Jack Williams" apparently did serve in the Thirteenth Cavalry because he was admitted to the Benton Barracks Hospital in November 1864 suffering from rheumatism—after Clayton's service was completed. The newspapers reported that fellow soldiers said Clayton was considered "a good fighting man," but everything else about her service appears to come from her own statements to the press.

Children were inevitably drawn into the war. They were witnesses to the depredations by soldiers and guerrillas visited on their homes, parents and siblings. Angeline and Lizzie McReynolds wrote to their brother describing their father Allen's death. Several men dressed as bushwhackers rode to the family farm. McReynolds was a confirmed secessionist and had provided help to guerrillas in the past. He took the men down the road to show them where Federal troops had passed. But the bushwhackers were Federal soldiers in disguise. Lizzie discovered her father had left the house and ran to find him. She was horrified when the soldiers shot him three times in the head and six times in the body and then kicked his lifeless corpse in the face. When McReynold's widow, Martha, wrote a letter to the newspapers detailing the crime, the secretary of war demanded an explanation. The captain who ordered the killing merely said that McReynolds was defiant in admitting his guilt. The soldiers were not punished.

Sometimes children themselves were the victims. Rachel Anderson recorded an incident in 1863 when a soldier forced young Bettie Skein to come with him at gunpoint. Fortunately, he was intercepted before any harm came to the girl, but she was "almost deranged" with fright and her invalid mother's life "despaired of."

Children frequently took a more active role by enlisting in the army, sometimes with their parents' consent and sometimes not. William Caton joined the Second Missouri Cavalry in October 1862, and his father, Aaron (already of member of the unit), signed the consent form certifying that William was seventeen. He was actually thirteen. Ludwick St. John enlisted in the Ninth Cavalry, MSM, supposedly at age eighteen. He was actually fourteen. Historian James Martens says that there were 10,233 soldiers in the United States Army alone that were under the age of eighteen, including 127 thirteen-year-olds.

Some children did not have to lie about their age. David Wood, son of Samuel Wood, was only ten years old when he joined his father's regiment, the Sixth Missouri Cavalry. The elder Wood was lieutenant colonel of the regiment and as an officer had the privilege of having his family accompany him. One day when on patrol,

Ten-year-old David Wood served as an orderly in his father's Sixth Missouri Cavalry until he became seriously ill. *Wilson's Creek National Battlefield.*

he heard a commotion behind him. He turned and saw young David in a group of soldiers. David's father gave in and let him enlist as a bugler. Samuel had his son with him as an orderly, primarily delivering messages rather than serving in the company to which he was assigned. David became seriously ill with malaria and pneumonia while stationed at Rolla in the summer of 1862. When his company was ordered to Helena, Arkansas, David stayed in Rolla with a farm family. Through either a mix-up or some unknown animosity, the company commander reported David as a deserter, and he received a dishonorable discharge. Upon his recovery, David went home to Kansas and never rejoined the army. David ran livery, feed and freight hauling businesses in Kansas and Colorado after the war. In later years, he managed silver mines. The secretary of war changed his discharge to an honorable discharge in 1912. David died in 1944 at age ninety-two.

8

WAR WEARINESS SETS IN: RURAL MISSOURI IN 1863–64

On June 16, 1863, Elvira Scott became embroiled in a confrontation far more frightening than the scrapes she and John had experienced in 1862. Fifty or sixty Federal soldiers rode into town, and the rumor spread that they were dreaded "Red Legs," Kansas cavalry noted for their red leather leggings (hence the nickname) and their fierce treatment of Missourians, no matter where their sympathies lay. Although these men probably were members of the Fourth Cavalry MSM then headquartered at Marshall, not Red Legs, their actions were disturbing enough.

Eight soldiers came to her house and demanded dinner. She provided it, being careful not to anger them. Just as she thought the crisis had passed, Elvira heard a commotion in the front yard. There she found John at gunpoint. She forced herself between the drunken soldier and her husband, and the three of them struggled as they got to the dining room door. She grabbed the soldier's arm. He kept threatening to shoot John until Elvira calmed him down. But she could not prevent the Federals from taking John prisoner, for the third time in a year, to Marshall, there to be held as hostage for the return of two Union men kidnapped (and later, as it happened, murdered) by guerrillas. Elvira set out the next day for Marshall to see about John's release, but she met him on the road. Still, the incident made up her mind: she and John must leave Miami for some place safer.

Before the Scotts could leave, however, more trouble came to town—this time in the form of guerrillas. A band led by George Todd visited Miami on August 3, 1863. Although sympathetic to their cause, the Scotts could not voluntarily give them supplies. John and a number of men in Miami were "under bond—they had promised not to aid the guerrillas—and so they told the guerrillas to take what they needed. One, a Dr. Graves, called for Elvira to fix him a meal. She declined, fearing that Union soldiers would find out and burn her house down. Graves replied, "Well, Madam, if you don't do it we will burn the house. You can take your choice." She chose to feed them. While in town, the guerrillas took some revenge. They killed three men, one of whom was known to have been a Union informant. Scott noted that the shooting of the other two was apparently a mistake and a "cruel, wicked deed," but as for the killing of the informant, "there was some excuse in his case."

By the end of the summer, Scott was sickened by both sides' conduct. Guerrillas and Union soldiers were killing one another and killing civilians thought to sympathize with the other side tit for tat. Guerrillas raided a "Dutch" town, stealing horses and money. Federals captured two men who admitted they were headed for the brush and hanged them. Guerrillas ambushed paymasters on their way to Lexington and Marshall, killing them, and in one instance were said to have stolen $50,000. "God help us," she wrote. "We are amid terrors on every side." Although John did not want to leave because people would think he was afraid, Elvira took matters into her own hands. Alone, she drove to Marshall to get a pass to go to St. Louis. On the way, she was confronted by a lone armed man, but he did no more than question her about "gorillas." It turned out that they needed no pass to leave. And so John left in early September 1863; Elvira boarded a steamboat about a week later.

Nancy Chapman Jones also grew weary of the war. Her initial enthusiasm had waned by October 1863. She complained that Shelby and his men were little better than the Federals in confiscating property. They took what they wanted from the stores in Boonville and not only ate the Jones's oats and corn, killed their cows and used their fence rails for their camp fires but also stole the family's last remaining horse.

The only excitement in town that did not involve the war revolved around the redoubtable Unionist Dr. Preston Beck. According to Jones, Dr. Beck concocted an elaborate scheme to woo the wealthy widow Broadhurst, a resident of nearby Howard County. In a letter recounting the delicious details, Jones wrote that Beck went to the Broadhurst farm and scouted out "a nice place to fall." The next day, his horse "threw" him on that very spot. Two of Broadhurst's slaves carried Dr. Beck, stunned speechless but otherwise miraculously unhurt, into the house. (Dr. Beck was said to have later slipped the two a twenty-dollar gold piece each.) There began a whirlwind affair, which ended a few days later with the uniting of the fortunes (financial and otherwise) in marriage—in the same room where only one month earlier Dr. Beck's first wife had died.

But these diversions were overshadowed by the increasingly vicious war. Murders were commonplace. It was time for the Jones family to go. They, however, did not merely relocate to St. Louis. Rather, they joined a sizable colony of Southern sympathizers in Canada to sit out the remainder of the war.

The war weakened slavery, as even strong Southern sympathizers such as Elvira Scott recognized it would. She noted the passage of the Second Confiscation Act and predicted that emancipation "seemed certain" in the border states. In her own household, Elvira's servant, Margaret, was acting "careless & impertinent."

Rachel King Anderson, a resident of Greene County, also recorded in her diary the hazards of living in rural Missouri ostensibly under Union control. On January 8, 1863, Rebels under General John Marmaduke attacked Springfield, throwing the entire county "into the wildest confusion." Three weeks later, her husband, William, left on one of his trips up the Wire Road to Rolla. While he was gone, soldiers repeatedly swept through the neighborhood foraging for food. They took corn and livestock. She was given receipts for the food that was taken, but receipts could not be eaten, and they were discounted by "shavers" who purchased them for about three-quarters of their value. Anderson never knew whether the soldiers would be friendly or not. On February 26, 1863, a company of cavalry "robbed all my hens nests, boiled the eggs in my milk bucket, stole my milk cups and plundered things generally." Two days later, four very well-behaved soldiers showed up near midnight calling for food and lodging.

On October 2, 1863, Anderson experienced "the darkest night of my life…I pray God no darker day or night may ever pass the horizon of my life." She recorded the details in her diary:

> *Between nine and ten o'clock last night just after we had gone to sleep, our faithful "old Turk" awaked us by a fierce and desperate barking. Mr. A and I both sprang out of bed at once. I looked out at the window and saw three men in Federal uniform all throwing rocks and beating the dog, and a man at the door demanding it to be opened. We opened the door and he entered, a bony faced man without beard, had on an old slouched white hat and grey coat with his revolver cocked and presented. He called out, "Strike a light and be damn quick." I demanded who and what they were when they only*

Rachel Young King Anderson, holding her diary. *Collection of Sally Conrad.*

swore at me to strike a light; a light was struck. He then demanded arms and finding none and knowing we had none, he then said, "You have green backs, you damn southern man, and we have come for it. I began to beg and cry out when he cursed me for a god damn fool and said if I did not get it quick he would blow Mr. Anderson's brains out. He looked so terrible and threatened so awful that I gave him what money we had on hand, some $65 or so. He counted it all over and swore we had more and he would have it and also demanded gold but as I have no doubt he knew before he came what money was on hand, he did not search anything except one satchel. I went to the door and cried out hoping to alarm the near neighbors. When the man outside darted back into the shade of the house and hedges and one of them a tall man swore at me

"Guerrilla Depredations—Seizing Horses," from *Harper's Weekly*, December 24, 1864. *Library of Congress.*

if I did not hush he would burn everything we had, but I still cried out until my daughter Belle sprang out of bed and clinging round my neck begged me to hush or they might kill her pa. They left in a hurry. We kept a light all night fearing they would return. At daylight we opened the door and old Turk rushed in and smelling all round found us all here. He jumped and reared and capered as though he was in an ecstacy of joy. It was enough to make us shed tears to look at his actions.

St. Louis became a magnet for refugees because of its location on the Mississippi River and because it was the nearest large city to the battlefields in Missouri, Arkansas and Tennessee that seemed safe. The first large wave—perhaps as many as forty thousand displaced persons—came in 1861. When Price defeated Lyon at Wilson's Creek, many residents in Southwest Missouri loaded up their belongings and made the long, difficult trip to Rolla and then to St. Louis. The influx of pitiful Missourians, plus the arrival of many runaway slaves, led to the first assessments against known or suspected Southern sympathizers.

That winter, a family from Fayetteville, Arkansas, made the long trek to St. Louis when Confederate authorities gave then ten hours to pack their belongings and head north. The grandfather had been born in the north and the son had disloyal—Northern—leanings. They were harassed and robbed on the way to the Missouri border. Finally, they reached Rolla, but several family members died on the trip, and the two remaining women died in camp there. Only the grandfather and a grandson made it all the way to St. Louis.

The flow of refugees never really stopped. In August 1862, George Wolz and the Third Cavalry MSM left Newtonia at sundown, accompanied by 2,500 refugees, including women and children, making the column about seven miles long. They marched all night. After stopping at 2:00 p.m. the next day to rest, the column once again made a night march toward Springfield—this time not stopping until ten o'clock the next morning. Wolz noted that there was "a good deal of murmuring about the way we left town and citizens," but he told his brother we "left By special order of General Brown" because the officers believed there were large columns of Confederates marching on Rolla, Springfield and Cassville.

The tale was repeated again in the winter of 1864. Ozias Ruark, a captain in the Eighth Cavalry MSM, recorded in his diary for February 26 that his men escorted a train of refugees from northern Arkansas that were "poor and nearly almost naked [and] some of the women and children barefooted." The next day, a heavy snow fell, and the column pushed through a dense pine forest. The women and children "suffered dreadfully." Ruark was moved to note that "men and angels pity the poor suffering women and children." Finally, they reached Forsyth on the White River. After a day of rest, Ruark's men pushed the refugees' wagons over the rugged hills until they reached Ozark. At that point, Ruark left the miserable group to make their way to Springfield, Rolla, St. Louis or wherever they intended to go.

Ruark did what he could to protect civilians—even Rebel civilians. His refusal to take cattle from enemy women and children in Southwest Missouri led to his men drawing up a petition to have him removed. His resignation was refused, however. By the summer of 1864, any semblance that guerrillas were respecting civilian rights was gone. Bushwhackers stole food, livestock and money from them; they burned homes, and they murdered anyone who resisted. Ruark noted that "the wailing and weeping" of one widow whose husband he helped bury was "heart rending."

But the largest single flight of white Americans from "friendly" territory during the war came in western Missouri in the late summer of 1863.

"The dark side of war—refugees from Southern Missouri, driven from their homesteads by the Rebels," *Frank Leslie's Illustrated Newspaper. Library of Congress.*

Guerrillas had increased their activities to the point that the new commander, General Thomas Ewing, needed to do something. He stationed his troops at a string of posts along the Missouri-Kansas border, but their role was more reactive than proactive. Ewing correctly diagnosed the secret to the guerrillas' success as being in large part due to the civilian support they received in the region. Ewing pointed out that the remaining civilians in Missouri's western counties "are kin to the guerrillas, and are actively and heartily engaged in feeding, clothing, and sustaining them. The presence of these families is the cause of the presence there of the guerrillas…They will, therefore, continue guerrilla war as long as they remain, and will stay as long as possible if their families remain." He sought permission to remove them, but before that could be done, William Quantrill led about four hundred men on a vicious raid on Lawrence, Kansas. The guerrillas killed over 150 men and boys in less than five hours.

Senator James Lane threatened to lead Kansas troops to lay waste to western Missouri. To his credit, Ewing forestalled that threat, but he replaced it with a notorious order of evacuation—Order No. 11. *All* persons in Jackson, Cass, Bates and northern Vernon Counties were to leave within fifteen days. Anyone approved as loyal could stay, but they had to move to military posts within the area for protection and so the army could keep an eye on them.

Thomas Ewing Jr. issued Order No. 11 requiring civilians in four counties in western Missouri to leave their homes within fifteen days. *Library of Congress*.

Most Union sympathizers had been driven out of the area by 1863. Thus, Order No. 11 fell most heavily on the women, children and elderly men who stayed behind when their husbands, fathers and sons joined the Confederate army or one of several guerrilla bands.

The exact number of persons affected is not known, but at least ten thousand and perhaps as many as twenty thousand persons packed their belongings and left for points east. Ewing, perhaps to mollify Lane but otherwise inexplicably, sent Kansas cavalry—the fiercely anti-Southern, anti-Missourian Red Legs (so-called for the red leather leggings they wore)—to carry out the order. No matter who enforced it, Order No. 11 was harsh, but the Red Legs made a tragic situation worse. Ewing issued orders against wanton pillaging, but they were largely ignored. Not only did those fleeing their homes have to share the crowded and dusty roads with a hostile force, but also the Kansans attacked many of them before they were even able to leave.

Lieutenant Colonel Bazel Lazear watched as the civilians streamed eastward, but with little sympathy:

> [T]*here is hundreds of people leaving their homes from this country and god knows what is to become of them. It is heart sickening to see what I have seen since I have been back here. A desolated country and women & children, some of them allmost naked. Some on foot and some in old wagons. Oh god. What a sight to see in this once peaceable and happy country.*

"Order No. 11," by Harry C. Edwards, from Caroline Abbot Stanley, *Order No. 11: A Tale of the Border*, 1904.

[Coming down from Kansas City on the boat I] *saw the secesh women and children and the few men fleeing from the wrath to come.... the boat was crowded full of them and god knows where they are all going for I dont nor do I care.*

The exodus was not just whites fleeing under Order No. 11. Large numbers of former slaves took advantage of the chaos to seize their freedom.

Escaped slaves entering Union lines. *Library of Congress.*

Elvira Scott recorded in her diary for August 31 that Miami was inundated by a wagon train "filled with Negro women & children" followed by nearly 250 men. They lacked food and shelter and thus immediately took over the empty homes of persons who had fled the war. The black refugees were as destitute as the white ones. Colonel George Hall wrote to his superior, General Egbert Brown, for assistance in feeding the runaways at Miami. Brown replied that the former slaves could go back home if they were hungry because the military was not going to provide them any food. So, to the disgust of Elvira Scott, the former slaves took whatever food they could find from gardens, chicken coops and pig pens in town.

Unionists fled before the guerrillas, and secessionists fled before the Federals. By 1863, much of the state was "nearly forsaken." Carthage and Nevada were reduced to ruins. Westport (near Kansas City) "was once a thriving town, with large stores, elegant private dwellings and a fine large hotel. Now soldiers are quartered in the dwellings and horses occupy the storerooms. The hotel was burned down three days ago. The houses are torn to pieces, plastering off, the mantles used to build fires, and doors unhinged."

There would be another year of violence before the guerrilla war petered out.

9

MEDICAL CARE AND THE WESTERN SANITARY COMMISSION

About 6:00 a.m. on August 10, 1861, John Ray and his family heard the first shots fired from what became known as Bloody Hill across Wilson Creek, about ten miles southwest of Springfield. The Ray house sat just off the Wire Road at the top of another hill. It was the local post office and served at one time as a stop on the Butterfield Overland Stage route.

Ray sat on his porch and watched Federal troops emerge from the dense brush surrounding the creek and move across his cornfield. While the bullets flew, Roxanna Ray and her seven children, along with their slave Rhoda Ray and her three children, took refuge in the house's cellar. Soon, Confederate soldiers arrived with wounded—lots of wounded. Every room of the house was filled with wounded men, and the yellow flag signifying it was a hospital and not to be fired upon was erected. Roxanna and Rhoda, and likely some of the older children, fetched water for the men while the surgeons and attendants treated them. No doubt the house was bloody from the open wounds and the inevitable amputations that followed. Many of the men were too injured to move and remained with the Rays for up to six weeks.

No one was prepared for the huge number of wounded and sick soldiers the war would create—not Roxanna and Rhoda Ray; not the town of Springfield, which shortly after the battle was described as a "vast hospital"; and not the city of St. Louis, which began its role as the principal medical center of the Western and Trans-Mississippi Theaters. Thousands of soldiers passed through Missouri on their way to war, and thousands returned suffering from grievous injuries, debilitating illnesses or both.

The Ray house, the only surviving building from the Battle of Wilson's Creek, was used as a hospital. *Wilson's Creek National Battlefield.*

In Springfield, the wounded from the battle filled up a hospital established in the courthouse, the Bailey House Hotel, churches and schools and, finally, thirty to forty private homes. Many of the women who remained in the town volunteered as nurses. A Confederate surgeon wrote, "The fair sex, God bless them, are doing all they can in the way of cooking, serving, and nursing for sick and wounded." Hundreds of Union wounded were put into wagons for the rough trip over rutted roads to Rolla, where they were placed on railroad cars for St. Louis. The city was not prepared to receive them. The New House of Refuge, opened only a few days earlier, was simply an empty building with no beds, stoves or nurses. The men were laid on the bare floor, many still in the bloody clothes they wore when hit and many with the rifle balls still in their bodies. Doctors and neighbors quickly gathered food and bedclothes. Several hundred more wounded arrived within a few days.

Among those who volunteered to care for the soldiers was Adaline Couzins, the wife of John Couzins, the St. Louis police chief. She gathered bandages, lint for packing wounds and clean underwear. This was just the beginning of Adaline Couzins's distinguished career as a nurse and medical provider to Civil War soldiers. Members of the Ladies Union Aid Society—mostly wives of merchants originally from the Northeast—also helped to provide medical care by rolling bandages, collecting clothing, reading and writing letters for injured and sick patients and providing other nursing services.

A St. Louis hospital, showing the 1864 United States flag. *Wilson's Creek National Battlefield.*

The city's elite pressured General Frémont to take action. Encouraged by his wife, Jessie, Frémont approved William Greenleaf Eliot's plans and authorized the creation of the Western Sanitary Commission on September 5, 1861. It opened the City General Hospital in September 1861 and five more in the next two months. By May 1862, the commission had fifteen hospitals with six thousand beds available and had treated nearly twenty thousand patients.

The Western Sanitary Commission became the principal civilian organization that not only supplemented military medical care but also provided relief supplies and services to refugees, white and black, that streamed into St. Louis from outstate Missouri, Arkansas and Tennessee.

The Western Sanitary Commission did not confine its activities to St. Louis or Missouri. A delegation led by Dr. Simon Pollak followed Grant's forces down the Tennessee and Cumberland Rivers. A number of prominent St. Louis women accompanied Pollak, but only two, he said, "were worth anything"—a Mrs. Kershaw and Adaline Couzins. While most of the women ("society imps," Pollak called them) were content with fanning the brows and reading to the wounded, Couzins and Kershaw "changed the bloody, torn and muddy garments of the wounded soldiers; bathed them; performed all kinds of menial work." Couzins's daughter, Phoebe, met her mother when the steamer brought the men back to St. Louis. It was full of "[m]aimed, bleeding, dying soldiers by the hundreds…and boxes—filled with amputated limbs, and dead awaiting their last rites." Adaline Couzins returned to Tennessee just in time for

"Campaign sketches. The letter for home," by Winslow Homer. *Library of Congress.*

the aftermath of the Battle of Shiloh. There she saw the horrific results of modern warfare—men shattered by artillery shell fragments and rifle balls, covered with mud and blood. Steamboats transported nearly 3,400 patients to St. Louis from Pittsburg Landing. Adaline Couzins would make repeated trips to the field, even suffering a wound herself from a Minié ball during the siege of Vicksburg.

In addition to medical care, the commission provided relief supplies and housing to the thousands of refugees who came to St. Louis. The first wave arrived in the late summer and early fall of 1861, fleeing Price's army from Southwest Missouri after the Battle of Wilson's Creek. The first round of assessments was made against Southern sympathizers to pay for the cost of housing, clothing and feeding these unfortunates. As the war dragged on, many former slaves fled their homes and came to the city to escape bondage. The women from the Ladies Union Aid Society organized a Ladies Freedmen's Relief Association that worked with the Freedmen's Relief Association to convert the Lawson Hospital into a home for black refugees and to create an orphanage for black children. A contraband camp was established at Benton Barracks. The group also provided a school for black children at the barracks in cooperation with the Western Sanitary Commission. When a separate hospital was opened for black troops at Benton Barracks in April 1864, a group of black women organized the Colored Ladies' Union Aid Society to assist them.

Among the innovations pioneered by the Western Sanitary Commission were "floating hospitals," steamboats fully equipped to follow the army down the western rivers to provide hospital care as near to the front as possible. The first boats were simply regular transports, but soon the commission had boats specially refitted to serve as hospitals. The best known was the *Red Rover*. It was a side-wheel steamer built in Louisville in 1857 and used by the Confederacy until it was captured at Island No. 10 in 1862. By May 1862 it was ready to join the Union fleet. The *Red Rover* had amputation and treatment rooms, three steam elevators to move patients between decks, a laundry, an icebox that held three hundred tons of ice, rooms for bathing, nine water closets, two kitchens and special blinds to keep out cinders from the smokestacks and insects. Unlike modern hospital ships, the *Red Rover* was armed; it carried a thirty-two-pounder cannon and small arms. Although it was prepared for battle on several occasions, it saw combat only once—on January 21, 1863, near Napoleon, Mississippi, a Rebel battery fired a cannon ball through its hospital ward, but no serious casualties were recorded. The ship had the distinction of having as part of its crew the first female nurses in the navy—nuns from the Sisters of Charity and at least five African American former slaves. The *Red Rover* supported army operations on the Mississippi at St. Charles, Arkansas, Memphis, Helena, Vicksburg and New Orleans, treating 1,697 patients.

The goods distributed and the money to pay for all of these activities of the Western Sanitary Commission primarily came from private donations.

The *Red Rover* was a "floating hospital" specially equipped by the Western Sanitary Commission to provide medical services close to Union lines. *Library of Congress.*

(The State of Missouri contributed $75,000, and St. Louis County gave $2,000.) The commission solicited funds from the entire country, not just the Middle and Upper Middle West. Indeed, its fundraising efforts in New England were one of the sore points in its relationship with the United States Sanitary Commission—in addition to the westerners' refusal to become subordinate to that group.

In the winter of 1861–62, the Ladies Union Aid Society had staged a series of *tableaux vivants* in the Mercantile Library with the most socially prominent women and girls. In these productions, the women emulated statues to represent classical scenes or incidents in history. Phoebe Couzins appeared in the *tableaux* along with the daughter of Truman Post, a Congregational minister originally from Middlebury, Vermont. Post's daughter was said to offer "a perfect Grecian profile" as the representation of the "Goddess of Liberty." In 1863, women decorated four rooms of the Lindell Hotel with flowers to represent the four seasons in a sylvan fête. Phoebe Couzins once again played an important role, this time leading the flower maidens as the Queen of Flowers in processions and dances.

But by 1864, the Western Sanitary Commission needed a new infusion of cash. The Ladies Union Aid Society suggested holding a sanitary fair. Other charitable organizations had successfully put on such fairs. In Chicago, for example, the United States Sanitary Commission had raised $80,000 in a twelve-day affair. The Mississippi Valley Sanitary Fair was organized at a meeting on February 1, at which speeches by the mayor, General Rosecrans, William Greenleaf Eliot and others were given. A number of committees were

Cover of sheet music for a polka composed for the Mississippi Valley Sanitary Fair of 1864 showing the main building. *Library of Congress.*

appointed to oversee the work, including a Standing Committee consisting of the five commissioners in charge of the Western Sanitary Commission, an Executive Committee of Gentlemen and an Executive Committee of Ladies. Phoebe Couzins, as befitted her philanthropic activity, was named the ladies' corresponding secretary. Her mother, Adaline, and a number of other prominent St. Louis women, including the wives of Frank Blair and Charles Drake, were also committee members.

Organizers built a temporary structure to house the main elements of the fair on Twelfth Street (now Tucker) between Olive and St. Charles Streets on the western edge of the business district. The building was 540 feet long and 114 feet wide, with two wings, each 100 feet long, extending along Locust Street. It had an octagon center 75 feet in diameter and 50 feet high decorated with mottoes, flags, battle trophies including two cannons captured at Vicksburg and flowers. It was divided into forty-seven "apartments" or sections for displays. On one side was a stereopticon projecting slides of realistic images used to tell stories—a precursor to the motion picture.

Men from the Sixty-eighth United States Colored Infantry helped construct the buildings for which they were paid fifty cents per day. The soldiers donated their wages plus "a very considerable addition" from their "scanty monthly pay" to a separate fund created by the fair's managers for freedmen relief.

The fair opened on May 17, with speeches and public celebrations. It opened to the public on May 18 and ran through June 18. Admission was two dollars on the opening day, one dollar the next two days and fifty cents after that. The fair featured restaurants, soda fountains, elaborate floral displays, a fortuneteller and a skating pond. The gallery of fine arts displayed a number of paintings and a wreath made of hair from the heads of generals and most of the president's cabinet "entwined in capillary union."

Among the biggest fundraisers were raffles. The most popular prize was Smizer's Farm, a five-hundred-acre place near Fenton in St. Louis County valued at $40,000, apparently confiscated for failure to pay assessments and donated by the county government. William Smizer was long suspected of secessionist sentiments. He refused to take the loyalty oath because he objected to its provision that the oath was "freely given." When soldiers visited the farm, the commander reported that Mrs. Smizer was "very mean," insulting the soldiers as "d____d dutch fools." Mrs. Smizer was banished in May 1863, along with a number of prominent Southern sympathizers. Fifty thousand tickets were sold at one dollar apiece; the farm was won by a Captain L.P. Martin from Iowa. A second raffle that drew much attention was the closing night's drawing for three bars of silver from Nevada valued at $4,000 each. Other prizes included a rosewood piano, a Turkish tiger rifle, a billiard table, horses and a model steamboat.

Organizers sent invitations to President Lincoln and General Ulysses Grant, but neither was able to attend due to pressing duties in the East. Grant was at that moment involved in the heavy fighting at Spotsylvania. His wife and children not only attended the fair but also were participants. Nellie, the Grants' nine-year-old daughter, played the role of the Old Lady Who Lived in a Shoe, surrounded by dolls representing her children. Julia Dent Grant recalled the event in her memoirs.

Nellie Grant sold dolls for fifty cents as the Old Lady Who Lived in a Shoe at the Mississippi Valley Sanitary Fair. *Ulysses S. Grant National Historic Site.*

Nellie was delighted with her metamorphosis, seated as she was in a mammoth black pasteboard shoe filled with beautiful dolls of all sizes. Nellie wore over her pretty curls a wide, ruffled cap and a pair of huge spectacles across her pretty, rosy, dimpled face. She was delighted with the selling of her dolls and pictures, telling me the ladies gave her a half dollar for every doll and every picture.

The fair accomplished everything its organizers hoped for. It provided an entertaining and educational diversion for a city and state grown weary of years of brutal warfare. And in monetary terms, it was an enormous success. The Executive Committee of Gentlemen (although women provided the impetus and much of the labor and goods sold, men still made the "important" decisions) reported the fair had gross receipts of $618,782 and a net profit of $554,591. Most of the revenues—$345,000—went to pay for medical supplies, clothing and other articles for use in the commission's hospitals and hospital boats. The Ladies Union Aid Society received $50,000 for its use in providing services to local hospitals. The fair gave $64,000 for the relief of refugees and freedmen. Another special fund for black refugees totaled $6,115, and the fair established a $1,000-per-month annuity for the Ladies Freedmen Relief Association. Proceeds of the fair were also used to establish a Soldiers' Orphan Home in Webster Groves.

The Western Sanitary Commission continued in existence after the war. It was finally disbanded in 1886 after the death of William Greenleaf Eliot, whose brainchild it was. The commission's remaining assets were donated to a nursing school named in his memory.

10

CONFRONTATION, EMANCIPATION AND THE IRONCLAD OATH

Although the Emancipation Proclamation issued on January 1, 1863, did not apply to Missouri because it was a loyal state, slaves in Missouri did not know or care about such distinctions. One of the points of contention between Governor Gamble and Samuel Curtis, who assumed duties as the new department commander in September 1862, was the enforcement of the provision of the Second Confiscation Act that freed slaves of persons known to be Rebels. Curtis's provost marshal, Franklin Dick, authorized the issuance of certificates of freedom to former slaves based only on their assertion that their master supported the rebellion. Once word of this policy became known, slaves began to leave for Union army camps in large numbers.

While the growing Radical faction approved of General Curtis, conservatives campaigned to have him replaced. Complaints over Curtis and Dick's assessments led to the suspension of the practice in January 1863. Conservatives circulated rumors, vehemently denied by Curtis, that he was involved in corrupt cotton trading. The relationship between Gamble and Curtis grew worse. Lincoln decided to replace Curtis, but the man he named, William Sumner, unexpectedly died before he could assume command. Finally, Lincoln brought back John Schofield as departmental commander in May 1863. He wrote to Schofield that he did not remove Curtis because he had done anything wrong. Rather, Lincoln said that the Union men in Missouri had fallen into a "pestilential factional quarrel" with Curtis at the head of one faction and Governor Gamble the other. "[A]s I could not

Samuel Curtis pursued antislavery policies in Missouri that conflicted with Governor Gamble's and led to his removal by Lincoln. *Library of Congress.*

remove Governor Gamble, I had to remove General Curtis." Lincoln went on to urge Schofield to follow a moderate course. "If both factions, or neither, shall abuse you, you will, probably, be about right."

Somehow Lincoln's letter got into Radical hands in Missouri, and it was published. Both conservatives and Radicals were incensed. Gamble wrote a blistering reply to the president, calling the reference to him a "most wanton and unmerited insult." Lincoln refused to read Gamble's letter "to preserve my own temper, by avoiding irritants, so far as practicable." He denied acting from any malice toward the governor.

Schofield suspected that Curtis had turned the letter over to the newspapers. (Curtis denied it.) Schofield summoned the editor, William McKee, to explain his actions, but he declined to appear. Schofield arrested McKee and demanded to know who provided the letter. McKee refused to divulge his source. At that point, Lincoln intervened and called Schofield's hunt off. "Please spare me the trouble this is likely to bring," he wrote. Schofield complied, but that did not settle the uproar.

Charles Drake, a newly minted Radical (he had been a Know-Nothing in the 1850s and a proslavery Democrat as late as 1860) led the emerging Radical Republicans, whose major platform plank was immediate and uncompensated emancipation of the slaves. Throughout 1863, Charles Drake repeatedly criticized Lincoln as too soft and as a dupe of conservatives like Gamble. The governor, he said, "was in fact in sympathy with the disloyal people of Missouri, however little you like it."

The disaster at Lawrence brought Missouri Radicals into another confrontation with the president, this time in person. Accompanied by Kansas senator James Lane, Drake led a delegation of seventy Missourians into the East Room of the White House, where they were introduced one by one to the president. John Hay, one of Lincoln's personal secretaries, took notes of the meeting. Hay, an Illinois native and a graduate of Brown University, had little use for the "frowsy" and "ungodly Pike"—a term of derision for Missourians. They were, Hay recorded, "[a]n ill combed, black broadcloth, dusty, longhaired and generally vulgar assemblage of earnest men who came to get their right as they viewed it."

Drake read a statement complaining of the ineptitude of General Schofield and seeking to have him replaced by the comfortably radical General Benjamin F. Butler. They also

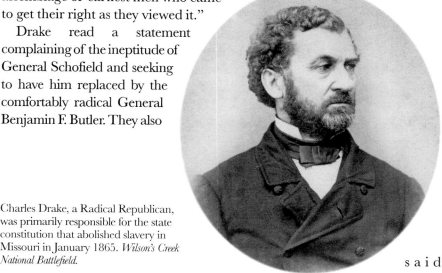

Charles Drake, a Radical Republican, was primarily responsible for the state constitution that abolished slavery in Missouri in January 1865. *Wilson's Creek National Battlefield.*

said

that the EMM was ineffective and largely disloyal and sought to have it replaced by regular Federal troops. Drake protested that Gamble had no authority to require men to join the EMM and that some Radicals who intended to file a lawsuit to that effect were prevented from doing so when General Schofield announced that the president's suspension of the writ of habeas corpus would apply in such cases.

Lincoln listened patiently. When Drake was finished, though, the president went on the attack. He pointed out that the criticisms of General Schofield were "vague denunciations" whose basis was his sympathy with their political enemies. He defended Schofield's administration of the department and praised him for sending much-needed reinforcements to Grant at Vicksburg. As for their complaints about the suspension of habeas corpus, he noted that their position was "that which is right when employed against [your] opponents is wrong when employed against yourselves." The interview lasted for an hour, with the president trading barbs with Drake, Lane and rude "members from the interior" of Missouri. Lincoln promised a thoughtful response.

Drake waited ten days in Washington for the president's answer. Lincoln wrote it five days after the meeting but did not send it until Drake was back in St. Louis. Perhaps he wanted to avoid another personal confrontation. The response was thoughtful, but hardly what Drake's delegation wanted. Lincoln repeated his defense of General Schofield, refused to disband the EMM (noting that his suspension of habeas corpus did apply to prevent Radical attempts to attack its legality in court) and rued the political discord among Missouri Unionists over the issue of slavery. He summed up the situation in typical pithy prose:

> *We are in civil war. In such cases there always is a main question; but in this case that question is a perplexing compound—Union and Slavery. It thus becomes a question not of two sides merely, but of at least four sides, even among those who are for the Union, saying nothing of those who are against it. Thus, those who are for the Union with, but not without slavery—those for it without, but not with—those for it with or without, but prefer it with—and those for it with or without, but prefer it without. Among these again, is a subdivision of those who are for gradual but not for immediate, and those who are for immediate, but not for gradual extinction of slavery. It is easy to conceive that all these shades of opinion, and even more, may be sincerely entertained by honest and truthful men. Yet, all being for the Union, by reason of these differences, each will prefer a different way of sustaining the Union.*

Lincoln's refusal to accede to the Radicals' demands was a setback for them. It was followed shortly by an unsuccessful campaign to replace the Missouri Supreme Court judges, appointed by Gamble in 1862, who were retained in office by a thin margin in the November elections. Charges of fraud were bandied about, apparently with some reason. One regiment returned 1,084 votes for the Radical candidates and only 5 for the incumbents. It is likely that the Radicals did enjoy overwhelming support in that unit—the difficulty was that it had only 726 eligible voters.

On a more satisfactory note, General Schofield finally fulfilled the promise of the Second Confiscation Act and Emancipation Proclamation that slaves could join the Union army. This was, of course, a touchy subject in Missouri. The first regiment organized in Missouri was designated the Third Arkansas Volunteer Infantry (Colored) to avoid rousing the sensibilities of loyal slaveholders. However, all but the staunchest proslavery advocate realized that the recruitment of black soldiers was inevitable.

Schofield's order provided that slaves who were accepted for the army would be given a certificate declaring that they were forever free. To placate their owners—at least those who were loyal—the government would allow them to claim $300 per man who volunteered. Schofield did not, however, permit recruiting officers to travel to the field for men. Rather, they were directed to set up offices in the towns. That meant that slaves who wished to join had to run away from their masters (or seek their consent). Contrary to orders, slave patrols were revived in some counties for the express purpose of preventing bondsmen from enlisting. Some officers took steps to actively discourage enlistments. In Mexico, for example, William Poillon (later an officer in the Sixty-eighth United States Colored Infantry) wrote to his friend Dr. James Martien (Jefferson Jones's nemesis) that a local lieutenant brought back a man from St. Louis who had been rejected by the army. The man's horror stories about African American soldiers who were suffering from "Cold, Starvation and death" were being used to discourage volunteers. (The stories were true.)

Despite the obstacles, the lure of freedom was too much to stop the male slaves from taking the opportunity to lose their bonds forever.

Spottswood Rice tried to run away in 1863, but he was caught by slave patrols. He agreed with his owner, Benjamin Lewis, not to run away again. Rice, however, had no intention of staying on Lewis's plantation. In February 1864, he enlisted in the United States Army, persuading ten of Lewis's slaves from Howard County to join him. Like many new recruits, he suffered from disease and saw no action (Rice developed chronic rheumatism, which

An unidentified African American soldier at Benton Barracks. Approximately 40 percent of male slaves of military age in Missouri joined the army. *Library of Congress.*

plagued him for the rest of his life). He served honorably as a hospital attendant in St. Louis until he was discharged in 1865.

Nancy Jones reported that three of her slaves, Speed, Ike and Willie, signed up, and that all but two of a neighbor's slaves did likewise. In all, more than three hundred men were recruited at Boonville alone by the end of 1863. Paula Stratton's man—also named Ike—left in December. Willard Mendenhall noted in his diary that black soldiers were being recruited in Lexington—"an outrage," in his opinion.

William Messley, another Howard County recruit, was listed as an engineer in civilian life. The twenty-two year-old Messley was quickly picked to be the first sergeant of his company of the Sixty-second United States Colored Infantry. He became seriously ill in 1864 and for undisclosed reasons was reduced in rank to sergeant. But on May 13, 1865, in the last battle of the Civil War at Palmetto Ranch, Texas (on the Rio Grande), Messley earned a promotion back to first sergeant for "gallantry in action."

But the soldiers' pride in their newfound freedom and military service to their country was often tempered by troubles at home. The statute that freed a black recruit also freed "his mother and his wife and children." But the families usually did not accompany them to the army, and they were left at the mercy of their former owner. Some of the masters and mistresses treated them badly. It must have been wrenching for Private Andrew Hogshead (also known as Andrew Valentine) to receive a letter from his wife, Ann, that read, "You do not know how bad I am treated. They are treating me worse and worse every day. Our child cries for you. Send me some money as soon as you can for me and my child are almost naked. My cloth is yet in the loom and there

William Messley, from Howard County, Missouri, was promoted to first sergeant for gallantry at the Battle of Palmetto Ranch, Texas. *Wilson's Creek National Battlefield.*

is no telling when it will be out. Do not send any of your letters to Hogsett [his former owner] especially those having money in them as Hogsett will keep the money."

The commanders of these men sought help for them. One reported that wives of Simon Williamson and Richard Beasley, soldiers from Franklin County in the Sixty-fifth United States Colored Infantry, "have again been whipped by their Masters unmercifully" and prevented them from going to the post office to pick up mail. If they did get mail, the master was "sure to whip them for it if he knows it." Lieutenant William Argo, Seventh Cavalry MSM, reported from Sedalia that the families of black soldiers were being driven from their masters' homes. He was directed to send them to the contraband camp at Benton Barracks established by General Schofield.

Hogshead, Williamson and Beasley all later died of disease in Louisiana.

Some soldiers did not passively endure maltreatment of their families. Spottswood Rice wrote to his daughter Mary in September 1864, assuring her that he had not forgotten her and that he would come to take her from her mistress, Kitty Digges of Glasgow. "I expect to have you. If Diggs dont give you up this Government will and I feel confident that I will get you Your Miss Kaitty said that I tried to steal you But I'll let her know that god never intended for man to steal his own flesh and blood." To Digges, he wrote:

> *I received a letter from Cariline telling me that you say I tried to steal to plunder my child away from you now I want you to understand that mary is my Child and she is a God given rite of my own and you may hold on to hear as long as you can but I want you to remembor this one thing that the longor you keep my Child from me the longor you will have to burn in hell...I want you to understand kittey diggs that where ever you and I meets we are enmays to each orthere I offered once to pay you forty dollers for my own Child but I am glad now that you did not accept it Just hold on now as long as you can and the worse it will be for you you never in you life befor I came down hear did you give Children any thing not eny thing whatever not even a dollers worth of expens now you call my children your pro[per]ty not so with me my Children is my own and I expect to get them and when I get ready to come after mary I will have bout a powrer and autherity to bring hear away and to exacute vengencens on them that holds my Child you will then know how to talke to me I will assure that and you will know how to talk rite too I want you now to just hold on to hear if you want to iff your conchosence tells thats the road go that road and what it will*

brig you to kittey diggs I have no fears about geting mary out of your hands this whole Government gives chear to me and you cannot help your self[.]

The Digges family was frightened and angry. Kitty Digges's brother, Frank Digges, was a prominent man in Glasgow. He was a lawyer and served as the town's postmaster for a time. Although a slaveholder, Digges was a strong Unionist. He was the provost marshal for the area for a couple of years. Therefore, he and his family expected that their voices would be heard by the Missouri high command. After receiving Rice's letter, Frank wrote to William Rosecrans, the department commander, with his complaints. He asked Rosecrans "to send the scoundrel" that wrote the letters away. Digges explained that Rice's daughter Mary was hired out by his sister to another person. Kitty asked him to let Mary go to St. Louis, but he refused. He had let the rest of Rice's family go and would send Mary whenever he was satisfied that her mother could support her. Whether Rosecrans intervened is not known, but Mary did join her family in St. Louis.

Although the Digges family escaped any attacks by Union soldiers, Spottswood Rice's former master Benjamin Lewis met with tragedy a month later. A brigade of Price's soldiers led by Jo Shelby captured Glasgow on October 15. The Confederates moved on the next day, and townsfolk must have been relieved to see them go. But guerrilla "Bloody Bill" Anderson led his men into town on October 21. According to a lurid account in the *New York Times*, Anderson burst into Mrs. Lewis's bedroom demanding that she reveal where her husband was hiding. She at first said she did not know but relented when Anderson threatened to burn the house down. The guerrillas seized Lewis and "proceeded for several hours with a series of acts which the demons inhabiting the lowest hell could not surpass in cruelty." Lewis was punched, pistol-whipped and beaten. The guerrillas shoved the barrel of their revolvers in his mouth and threatened to blow his head off. Lewis offered them $1,000 in silver, but they demanded $5,000 in gold. A nighttime visit to the bank of Thompson & Dunnica produced the $5,000 in gold and greenbacks—Thompson being Lewis's cousin. While Anderson was torturing Lewis, some of his men were raping a young female slave. Early the next morning, the men returned and raped two more slave women. Lewis's health was broken. He survived the war but died shortly thereafter from the effects of his night of terror.

Missouri Radicals, led by Charles Drake, initially opposed Lincoln's reelection but later united behind him when their favorite, John C. Frémont,

Glasgow, Missouri, in 1864. Glasgow was an important port for the processing and shipping of tobacco. *Library of Congress.*

withdrew from the race. In the November 1864 election, the Radicals won control of the statehouse and both houses of the General Assembly, and they dominated the delegates to a state convention selected to draw up a new constitution. The convention's first order of business was the emancipation of slaves. There was no more debate about gradual versus immediate emancipation or whether the slaveholders should be compensated. Slavery had broken down in the state by the end of 1864, with little remaining but to give it a formal burial. On January 11, 1865, the convention approved emancipation of all slaves in Missouri effective July 4, 1865. When the news reached the Radical legislature, its members broke into a rousing rendition of "John Brown's Body." Dr. John Bates Johnson, a member of the Western Sanitary Commission, wrote of the celebrations in St. Louis:

> [W]e have had nothing but salutes, bonfires, illuminations and huzzas. The negroes are about the happiest mortals I have seen. They all seem calm, not disposed to any outbreak as evidence of their joy, but their faces seem lit up with new hope that they are free.

Emancipation Ordinance abolishing slavery in Missouri, January 11, 1865. *Library of Congress.*

Another major provision Drake sought to have in the new state constitution was the "ironclad" oath requiring anyone who sought to vote or to serve as a public official, juror, lawyer, corporate officer, trustee, teacher or minister to attest that he had not committed any of eighty-six actions in support of the rebellion. These innovations did not last long. The latter provision was declared unconstitutional by the United States Supreme Court in 1867 as a bill of attainder—punishment without a judicial trial. Frank Blair challenged the voting provision by refusing to take the oath—no one thought that a former Union major general and United States congressman supported the rebellion. In a surprise, the Supreme Court upheld the suffrage provision in a tie vote. But when former Confederates won the right to hold public office, these kinds of restrictions were repealed, and conservative Democrats once again controlled the state.

Epilogue

Once full civil rights were restored to Southern sympathizers and former Confederates, many were elected or reelected to public office. Among them was Jefferson Jones, now a postwar railroad promoter, who was returned to the state legislature as a representative from the "Kingdom of Callaway."

John Henderson served as a United States senator until 1869. He, along with six other Republicans, broke ranks to vote against conviction of President Andrew Johnson in his impeachment trial. In 1875, Henderson was appointed a special prosecutor to try defendants in the Whiskey Ring scandal during the Grant Administration. A number of prominent Republicans—including General Orville Babcock, President Grant's close friend and secretary—were accused of skimming tax revenues from the sale of whiskey. St. Louis was the center of the ring, but it had conspirators in several major cities. When Grant took steps that appeared to be motivated by the desire to protect Babcock, Henderson protested that the president was interfering with the prosecutions. Grant fired him. Henderson moved to Washington, D.C., in 1888.

Elvira and John Scott returned to Miami on June 21, 1865. There they stayed for the rest of their lives. Elvira had difficulty getting used to the status of newly freed slaves. She had to take over some household duties herself and hired African American women to do the rest. She was not satisfied with either their attitude or their work habits. To make matters worse, Elvira's antislavery sister Julia came from Iowa to stay with her. Julia made sure that the former slaves at the house were aware of the significance of their new status, to Elvira's annoyance. It was a relief when Julia finally left.

John died in 1888. Elvira took over management of the business and ran it successfully for many years. She wrote that "painting is my passion & I believe my talent." In the last decade of her life, she produced a number of works that hung in her house and those of her neighbors. Some of her paintings were exhibited at the St. Louis World's Fair in 1904. Elvira Scott died December 8, 1910.

Lizzie Powell moved to Virginia City, Nevada Territory, in 1864. There she met Alfred Hereford. They moved back to Missouri briefly after the war but soon moved again to Denver. In 1877, Lizzie Powell Hereford was returning from a drive with Mrs. John Routt, wife of the Colorado governor, when she was thrown from the carriage and sustained injuries that led to her death.

After her service for the Western Sanitary Commission, Phoebe Couzins entered into a profession that was almost exclusively the domain of men—the practice of law. She entered the law school at Washington University and was admitted to the bar in 1871. Couzins became involved in the movement for women's rights. She gave a speech for women's suffrage at the 1876 Democratic Convention in St. Louis. President Grover Cleveland appointed her father the United States marshal for the Eastern District of Missouri. After his death, President Cleveland appointed her to the post—the first woman ever to be a United States marshal. In later years, Couzins had a falling out with other suffragettes. She became crippled with arthritis and suffered from emotional instability. Couzins died in 1913 and was buried with her marshal's badge on.

Spottswood Rice remained in St. Louis after the war. State law required former slaves to formalize their marriages, and Spottswood and Arry did so in October 1864. Their daughter Mary did make it to St. Louis despite the objections and excuses of Kitty Digges. Rice founded the St. Peter AME Church in St. Louis, which remains active to this day. Arry died in 1888. Spottswood remarried the next year and moved to Albuquerque, New Mexico, where he founded yet another AME church, the Grant Chapel. A few years later, they moved to Manitou, Colorado, where he founded a third church, the Payne Chapel. Spottswood Rice died on October 31, 1907. Mary remained in St. Louis, where she was interviewed by the Federal Writer's Project in 1937 about her life and her parents' lives as slaves.

Moses and Susan Carver obviously loved young George and his brother Jim very much. The Carvers moved George and Jim into their house and raised them as if they were their own children. George longed to know more about his mother, but there was little to tell. He cherished into adulthood her spinning wheel and the bill of sale by which Moses had acquired ownership of her.

Although Jim was tall and robust, George was always frail and sickly. But he had a keen curiosity and a tenaciousness to learn. The Carvers sent the boys to school in nearby Neosho when George was about twelve, but it provided only the most basic instruction. He spent the next decade moving from Missouri to Kansas to Minnesota, trying to find his niche. Finally, he moved to Ames, Iowa, to attend what is now Iowa State University. There he found his calling: botany. He was invited to head the Agriculture Department at Tuskegee Institute by Booker T. Washington. Over the next forty-seven years, George became a world-renowned scientist, researcher, inventor and teacher. He became famous for his research into soil conservation and the use of peanuts. By the time of his death in 1943, George Washington Carver was one of the most well-known African Americans in the United States. The Carver farm near Diamond, Missouri, was declared a National Monument—the first such honor for an African American.

The soldiers and guerrillas returned to their homes and for the most part tried to resume their normal lives, but much of the bitterness and violence that accompanied the conflict continued. The saddest legacies of the war were the widows and orphans left by the estimated 700,000 soldiers who died in battle and from disease. (No one knows how many civilians died in the guerrilla war, but the number must be substantial.) Their only consolation was perhaps a photograph and a packet of letters.

George Washington Carver (left) and Jim Carver. *George Washington Carver National Monument.*

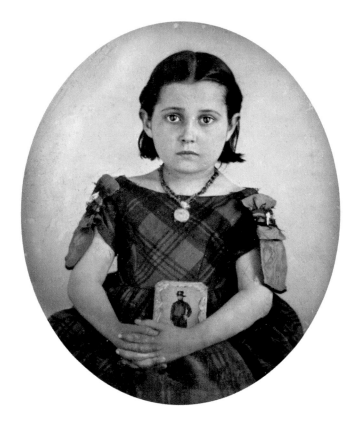

An unidentified girl in mourning holding a photograph of her father, an officer in the Union cavalry, who died in the war. *Library of Congress.*

As a partial recompense, the United States government provided a monthly pension for survivors of Union soldiers amounting to one-half of the soldier's monthly pay—for a private's children, it was eight dollars per month until age sixteen. Survivors of Confederate soldiers received no federal help. Missouri finally voted to provide a pension to Confederate soldiers, but not their survivors, in 1911. Theda Skocpol found that about one-quarter of all Missourians—former soldiers and survivors—were receiving a Civil War pension in the years before World War I. These pensions were the first large social welfare program in the United States.

BIBLIOGRAPHY

Anderson, Rachel Young King. *Diary, 1861–1865*. Collection of Sally Conrad.

Annual Report of the Adjutant General of Missouri, 1865. Jefferson City, MO: Emory S. Foster, Public Printer, 1866.

Basler, Roy P., ed. *Collected Works of Abraham Lincoln*. Vol. 6. New Brunswick, NJ: Rutgers University Press, 1953.

Beilein, Joseph M., Jr. "'The Presence of These Families Is the Cause of the Presence There of the Guerrillas': The Influence of Little Dixie Households on the Civil War in Missouri." Master's thesis, University of Missouri, 2006.

Berlin, Ira, Barbara J. Fields, Thavolia Glymph, Joseph P. Reidy and Leslie Rowland, eds. *Freedom: A Documentary History of Emancipation, 1861–1867*. Series I, Volume I, *The Destruction of Slavery*. Cambridge, UK: Cambridge University Press, 1985.

Berlin, Ira, Steven F. Miller, Joseph P. Reidy, and Leslie Rowland, eds. *Freedom: A Documentary History of Emancipation, 1861–1867*. Series I, Volume II, *The Wartime Genesis of Free Labor*. Cambridge, UK: Cambridge University Press, 1993.

Biographical Sketches of Newton County Families and Their Neighbors. Vol. 1. Neosho, MO: Genealogy Friends of the Library, 1992.

Blanton, DeAnne, and Lauren M. Clark. *They Fought Like Demons: Women Soldiers in the American Civil War*. Baton Rouge: Louisiana State University Press, 2002.

Boman, Dennis K. *Lincoln and Citizens' Rights in Civil War Missouri: Balancing Freedom and Security.* Baton Rouge: Louisiana State University Press, 2011.

Bowen, Don R. "Guerrilla War in Western Missouri, 1862–1865: Historical Extensions of the Relative Deprivation Hypothesis." *Comparative Studies in Society and History* 19, no.1 (January 1977).

Brannock, Lizzie. "Letter to Dear Brother Edwin, January 13, 1864." State Historical Society of Missouri, Columbia, Missouri, available at http://statehistoricalsocietyofmissouri.org/cdm/ref/collection/amcw/id/12442.

Brophy, Patrick, ed. *In the Devil's Dominions: A Union Soldier's Adventures in "Bushwhacker Country."* Nevada, MO: Vernon County Historical Society, 1998.

Buffon, Dianne, and Linda Brown-Kubisch, eds. *Report of the Committee of the House of Representatives of the General Assembly of the State of Missouri Appointed to Investigate the Conduct and Management of the Militia, Including an Index.* Columbia: State Historical Society of Missouri, 1998.

Burke, Diane Mutti. *On Slavery's Border: Small-slaveholding Households, 1815–1865.* Athens: University of Georgia Press., 2010

Burlingame, Michael, ed. *At Lincoln's Side: John Hay's Civil War Correspondence and Selected Writings.* Carbondale: Southern Illinois University Press, 2000.

Carter, Gari, ed. *Troubled State: Civil War Journals of Franklin Archibald Dick.* Kirksville, MO: Truman State University Press, 2008.

Castel, Albert, and Tom Goodrich. *Bloody Bill Anderson: The Short, Savage Life of a Civil War Guerrilla.* Lawrence: University Press of Kansas, 1998.

City Directory for St. Louis, Missouri. St. Louis: Gould Directory Co., 1888.

Cross, Jasper W. "The Mississippi Valley Sanitary Fair, St. Louis, 1864." *Missouri Historical Review* 46 (April 1952): 245.

Dew, Charles B. *Apostles of Disunion: Southern Secession Commissioners and the Causes of the Civil War.* Charlottesville: University Press of Virginia, 2001.

Dobak, William A. *Freedom By The Sword: The U.S. Colored Troops, 1862–1867.* New York: Skyhorse Publishing, 2013.

Earle, Jonathan, and Diane Mutti Burke, eds. *Bleeding Kansas, Bleeding Missouri: The Long Civil War on the Border.* Lawrence: University Press of Kansas, 2013.

Ewing, Ellen Cox. "Letter to Jinnie and Auntie, August 20, 1862." In *Ellen Cox Ewing Papers*, Pearce Civil War Collection, Navarro College, Corsicana, Texas. Available at http://www.ozarkscivilwar.org.

Fellman, Michael. *Inside War: The Guerrilla Conflict in Missouri During the American Civil War.* Oxford, UK: Oxford University Press, 1989.

Filbert, Preston. *The Half Not Told: The Civil War in a Frontier Town.* Mechanicsburg, PA: Stackpole Books, 2001.

Ford, James Everitt. *History of Grundy County*. Trenton, MO: News Publishing Company, 1908.

Forman, Jacob G. *The Western Sanitary Commission: A Sketch of Its Origin, History, Labors for the Sick and Wounded of the Western Armies, and Aid Given to Freedmen and Union Refugees, With Incidents of Hospital Life*. St. Louis: R.P. Studley & Co., 1864.

Frazier, Margaret Mendenhall, ed. *Missouri Ordeal, 1862–1864: Diaries of Willard Hall Mendenhall*. Newhall, CA: Carl Boyer III, 1985.

Fyfer, J. Thomas. *History of Boone County*. St. Louis: Western Historical Company, 1882.

Gallagher, Gary. *The Union War*. Cambridge, MA: Harvard University Press, 2011.

Geiger, Mark W. *Financial Fraud and Guerrilla Violence in Missouri's Civil War, 1861–1865*. New Haven, CT: Yale University Press, 2010.

Gerteis, Louis S. *Civil War St. Louis*. Lawrence: University of Kansas Press, 2001.

Grant, Julia Dent. *The Personal Memoirs of Julia Dent Grant*. Carbondale: Southern Illinois University Press, 1975.

Grasty, John S. *Memoir of Rev. Samuel B. McPheeters*. St. Louis, MO: Southwestern Book and Publishing Company and Davidson Brothers and Company, 1871.

Hacker, J. David. "A Census-Based Count of the Civil War Dead." *Civil War History* 57, no. 4 (December 2011): 307.

Harris, NiNi. *A Most Unsettled State*. St. Louis: Reedy Press, 2013.

Harris, William C. *Lincoln and the Border States*. Lawrence: University Press of Kansas, 2011.

Henkin, David M. *The Postal Age: The Emergence of Modern Communications in Nineteenth-Century America*. Chicago: University of Chicago Press, 2006.

History of Howard and Chariton Counties, Missouri. St. Louis: National Historical Company, 1883.

History of Lafayette County, Missouri. St. Louis: Missouri Historical Company, 1881.

History of Saline County, Missouri. St. Louis: Missouri Historical Company, 1881.

Holcombe, Return I. *History of Greene County*. St. Louis: Western Historical Company, 1883.

Hunter, Louis C. *Steamboats on the Western Rivers: An Economic and Technological History*. New York: Dover Publications, Inc., 1993.

Hurt, R. Douglas. *Agriculture and Slavery in Missouri's Little Dixie*. Columbia: University of Missouri Press, 1992.

Jackson, Robert W. *Rails Across the Mississippi: A History of the St. Louis Bridge*. Urbana: University of Illinois Press, 2001.

Jones, Nancy Chapman. *Letters*. State Historical Society of Missouri, Columbia, Missouri, available at http://statehistoricalsocietyofmissouri. org/cdm/compoundobject/collection/amcw/id/10829/rec/1.

Kiner, F.F. *One Year's Soldiering*. Lancaster, IA: E.H. Thomas, Printer, 1863.

Lass, William E. *Navigating the Missouri, Steamboating on Nature's Highway 1819–1935*. Norman: University of Oklahoma Press, 2008.

Lause, Mark A. *Price's Lost Campaign: The 1864 Invasion of Missouri*. Columbia: University of Missouri Press, 2011.

Lecture Flyer, *Mrs. F.L. Clatin*, Ephemera Invitation 0520, Record ID 379397, American Antiquarian Society. First printed on February 23, 1865.

Lothrop, Charles A. *A History of the First Regiment Iowa Cavalry, Veteran Volunteers*. Lyons, IA: Beers & Eaton, Printers, 1890.

Martens, James. *Children for the Union: The War Spirit on the Northern Front*. Chicago: Ivan R. Dee, 2004.

McArthur, Marcus. "Treason in the Pulpit: The Problem of Apolitical Preaching in Civil War Missouri." *Journal of Church and State* 53, no. 4 (2011): 545.

McCandless, Perry. *A History of Missouri: Volume II, 1820 to 1860*. Columbia: University of Missouri Press, pap. ed. 2000.

McLarty, Vivian Kirkpatrick, ed. "The Civil War Letters of Colonel Bazel F. Lazear." *Missouri Historical Review* 44 (July 1950): pt. 2, 387.

McMurray, Linda. *George Washington Carver, Scientist and Symbol*. New York: Oxford University Press, 1982.

Miami (MO) Weekly News, December 16, 1910.

Missouri Division, United Daughters of the Confederacy. *Reminiscences of the Women of Missouri During the Sixties*. Dayton, OH: Morningside House, Inc., 1988.

Missouri Slave Narratives: A Folk History of Slavery in Missouri from Interviews with Former Slaves from the Federal Writers' Project, 1936–1938. Bedford, MA, n.d.

National Archives and Records Administration. *Compiled Service Records of Volunteer Union Soldiers Who Served in Organizations from the State of Missouri*. Record Group 94; Microfilm: M405, various rolls.

———. *Union Provost Marshal's File of Papers Relating to Individual Civilians*. Record Group 109, M345, various rolls.

Neely, Mark, Jr. *The Fate of Liberty: Abraham Lincoln and Civil Liberties*. New York: Oxford University Press, 1991.

New York Times, February 16, 1862.

———, May 22, 1863.

———, November 2, 1864.

Northway, Martin. "The Prince Behind the Kingdom of Callaway County." *Missouri Life*, October 12, 2012. Available at http://www.missourilife. com/life/the-prince-behind-the-kingdom-of-callaway-county.

Oakes, James. *Freedom National: The Destruction of Slavery in the United States, 1861–1865*. New York: W.W. Norton & Company, Inc., 2013.

Parrish, William E. *The Civil War in Missouri; Essays from the Missouri Historical Review*. Columbia: State Historical Society of Missouri, 2006.

————. *History of Missouri, 1860 to 1875*. Columbia: University of Missouri Press, 2001.

————. *Missouri Under Radical Rule, 1865–1870*. Columbia: University of Missouri Press, 1965.

————. *Turbulent Partnership: Missouri and the Union, 1861–1865*. Columbia: University of Missouri Press, 1963.

Petition of Citizens of Balltown, Missouri, September 28, 1863, WICR 30903, parts 1–4, Wilson's Creek National Battlefield Museum.

Piston, William Garrett and Richard W. Hatcher III. *Wilson's Creek: The Second Battle of the Civil War and the Men Who Fought It*. Chapel Hill: University of North Carolina Press, 2000.

Piston, William Garrett, and Thomas P. Sweeney. *Portraits of Conflict: A Photographic History of Missouri in the Civil War*. Fayetteville: University of Arkansas Press, 2009.

Piston, William Garrett, ed. *A Rough Business: Fighting the Civil War in Missouri*. Columbia: State Historical Society of Missouri, 2012.

Quiner, E.B. *Quiner's Military History of Wisconsin*. Chicago: Clarke, 1866.

Rable, George C. *God's Almost Chosen Peoples: A Religious History of the American Civil War*. Chapel Hill: University of North Carolina Press, 2010.

Raymond, Steve. *In the Very Thickest of the Fight: The Civil War Service of the 78th Illinois Volunteer Infantry Regiment*. Guilford, CT: Globe Pequot Press, 2012.

Report of the North Missouri Railroad Company, Appendix, Exhibit B. Reprinted in *Journal of the Senate of Missouri, Twenty-Second General Assembly*. Jefferson City, MO: J.P. Ament, 1863.

Riddle, Donald W., ed. *A Diary of the Civil War on the Missouri Border* [Elvira Weir Scott Diary, 1860–1887]. State Historical Society of Missouri, Columbia, Missouri. Available at http://statehistoricalsocietyofmissouri. org/cdm/ref/collection/amcw/id/12308.

Roca, Steven Louis. "Presence and Precedents: The USS Red Rover during the American Civil War, 1861–1865." *Civil War History* 44, no. 2 (June 1998): 91.

Ruark, Ozias. *Diary, 1864–1865*. State Historical Society of Missouri, Columbia, Missouri. Available at http://statehistoricalsocietyofmissouri. org/cdm/compoundobject/collection/amcw/id/9892/rec/2.

Scharf, J. Thomas. *History of St. Louis City and County*. Vol. 1. Philadelphia: Louis H. Everts & Co., 1883.

Skocpol. Theda. *Protecting Soldiers and Mothers: The Political Origins of Social Policy in the United States*. Cambridge, MA: Belknap Press of Harvard University Press, 1992.

Smith, W. Wayne. "An Experiment in Counterinsurgency: The Assessment of Confederate Sympathizers in Missouri." *Journal of Southern History* 35, no. 3 (August 1969): 363.

Stillwell, Leander. *The Story of a Common Soldier of Army Life in the Civil War, 1861–1865*. N.p.: Franklin Hudson Publishing Co., 1920.

Sturgeon, Isaac N. "Reminiscences." In *Isaac H. Sturgeon Papers*. St. Louis: Missouri History Museum.

Troy (MO) Herald, October 28, 1874.

Volpe, Vernon L. "The Frémonts and Emancipation in Missouri." *Historian* 56, no. 2 (Winter 1994): 33.

Waal, Carla, and Barbara Oliver Korner, eds. *Hardship and Hope: Missouri Women Writing about Their Lives, 1820–1920*. Columbia: University of Missouri Press, 1997.

The War of the Rebellion: A Compilation of the Official Records of the Union and Confederate Armies. Washington, D.C.: United States Government Printing Office, 1880–1901.

Way, Frederick Jr. *Way's Packet Directory, 1848–1994*. Athens: Ohio University Press, rev. ed. 1983.

Whites, Leeann. "Forty Shirts and a Wagonload of Wheat: Women, the Domestic Supply Line, and the Civil War on the Western Border." *Journal of the Civil War Era* 1 (2011): 56.

Williams, Walker, ed. *History of Northeast Missouri*. 3 vols. Chicago: Lewis Publishing Company, 1913.

Winter, William C. *The Civil War in St. Louis: A Guided Tour*. St. Louis: Missouri Historical Society Press, 1994.

Wolz, George. "Letter to John Wolz, August 4, 1862." In *George Wolz Papers*. St. Louis: Missouri History Museum.

Wood, Larry. *Civil War Springfield*. Charleston, SC: The History Press, 2011.

Index

INDEX

ABOUT THE AUTHOR

James W. Erwin is a Missouri native. He graduated from Missouri State University with a BA in mathematics. After service in the United States Army, he obtained an MA in history from the University of Missouri and a JD from the University of Missouri Law School. He practiced law in St. Louis for more than thirty-seven years. Mr. Erwin is married to Vicki Berger Erwin. They live in Kirkwood, Missouri.